T0293923

What Days Are For

Also by Robert Dessaix

Fiction
Night Letters: a Journey through Switzerland and Italy
Corfu

Non-fiction
A Mother's Disgrace
Secrets with Drusilla Modjeska and Amanda Lohrey
(and so forth)
Twilight of Love: Travels with Turgenev
Arabesques: a Tale of Double Lives
On Humbug
As I Was Saying: a Collection of Musings

Edited
Picador New Writing
Australian Gay and Lesbian Writing: an Anthology
Speaking Their Minds: Intellectuals and the
Public Culture in Australia
The Best Australian Essays 2004
The Best Australian Essays 2005

What Days Are For
ROBERT DESSAIX

KNOPF

A Knopf book
Published by Random House Australia Pty Ltd
Level 3, 100 Pacific Highway, North Sydney NSW 2060
www.randomhouse.com.au

First published by Knopf in 2014

A preliminary version of short sections from chapters 1 and 8 were included in a speech given by the author at several writers' festivals in 2012–13; and from chapter 7 in *Best Australian Essays 2013*.

The author and publisher are grateful to Faber & Faber Ltd for permission to reproduce lines from 'Days' and 'The Old Fools' by Philip Larkin.

Addresses for companies within the Random House Group can be found at www.randomhouse.com.au/offices

National Library of Australia
Cataloguing-in-Publication entry

Dessaix, Robert, author
What days are for / Robert Dessaix

ISBN 9780857985767 (hardback)

Dessaix, Robert, 1944
Dessaix, Robert, 1944–Anecdotes
Essays.

A828.3

Cover and endpaper images © Stocksy
Cover design by Natalie Winter
Typeset in Palatino by Midland Typesetters, Australia
Printed in Australia by Griffin Press, an accredited ISO AS/NZS 14001:2004 Environmental Management System printer

Random House Australia uses papers that are natural, renewable and recyclable products and made from wood grown in sustainable forests. The logging and manufacturing processes are expected to conform to the environmental regulations of the country of origin.

To Susan Varga
and to the sixty years of our friendship

1

Sunday night

His face beams down at me like God's from a dome of bright light. Everything gleams. Every blond hair on his tanned forearm glistens as he fits my mask. It's a glossy, muscled forearm, used to hefting bodies. I've always been very taken with forearms, and this is a singularly lustrous, sinewy example. 'So, tell me, Robert,' he says gently, somewhere high up there inside his dome of dazzling light – am I already dead? No, not yet, soon – 'have you had a good day?'

A good day? I give a muffled laugh, batting away the pain blossoming in my chest. (*Apart from that,*

Mrs Lincoln, how did you enjoy the play? Tom Lehrer, wasn't it?) They're losing me, these two paramedics in their fluorescent jackets, and they know it – even I know I'm teetering on the edge of a big moment – and all the one with the burnished forearm can come up with is 'Have you had a good day?' It's surreal. The doors of the hotel foyer hiss open and a man, a woman and two teenaged children burst in out of the cold, squawking with late-night excitement, catch sight of the trolley, the body and the yellow jackets and hurry off towards the lifts.

'You know,' I croak, as if it were a serious question, as if he really wanted to know, 'I have. I've had a very good day.' And I have. I've walked the dog by the river, I remember, I've reread my play script aloud to myself in the sun, flown off with it at dusk across the sea to Sydney, mooched about (I'd have liked to frisk) in the gritty trashiness of Oxford Street (still rumbling and screeching out there beyond the plate-glass windows) . . . oh, and other things as well, I've enjoyed lots of other things, now I cast my mind back. Would he want to know the details?

'Well, that's wonderful,' he says, still gleaming, 'that's what matters.' Really? This sounds unlikely. But before I can pick an argument with him, they are trundling me out into the night, I am spasming with cold, a siren is screaming, I glide through doors, there's a lot of shouting, I slew left, I slew right, there are dozens of jarring voices, I feel clawed at by all the voices, but for some reason (and I know it's strange even as it's happening) they are all like noises-off. My mind is focused on the gleaming forearm and the voice from up inside the dome of light: 'Have you had a good day?'

Nobody, by the way, during this not so much interminable as boundless night asks if I've had a good weekend, let alone a good life. None of the voices jabbing at me ever asks what I think I've achieved in the course of my life or if I feel it's all been worthwhile (on the whole, all things considered). Nor do I ask myself these questions. Nobody cares at a time like this – why would anybody care? – about what I'd like to achieve if they can keep me going for a bit longer. Not a syllable, naturally, about whether or not I finally got to the bottom of things before the curtain started to come down, as I rather hoped to do – indeed, half-expected to do; surely it was just a matter of a week or two of the right kind of fallow time – but never did. (On the contrary, the older I get, the less sense anything makes.) Needless to say, nobody checks to see if I finally finished the Proust, as I vowed I would before I died, or learnt Sanskrit or the tango or made it to Bhutan. The only question anyone asks me is whether or not I've had a good day.

Well, on reflection, that's not *quite* true: coming to on this gurney or that, during this night that now seems beyond all thought of a beginning or an ending, I find myself being asked a few questions about who I am, whether or not I have private insurance and if there is somebody they should get in touch with. Imagine if at my age, after a lifetime of intimacies, there were absolutely no one! What would that say about me?

'Yes, there is,' I mumble, 'but tonight he's on a ferry in the middle of Bass Strait.' At some point I seem to remember signing something: in the eerie, arctic cold of some brightly lit white room (it's like being on a film set) I stretch out my hand and sign a form.

When more lucidly present, I become surprisingly talkative, sliding into my gracious-guest role, even offering a little light conversation. 'So, how are we going here?' I ask affably at one juncture, unaware I've already had to be resuscitated twice and am now bleeding to death. So much brilliant light everywhere. So many voices. But no faces, I can't see any faces. 'A little way to go yet,' someone says with a chuckle. Nicely put. Could mean anything, and does.

What I am mostly doing is drowning in vibrantly coloured dreams. I am pixilating woozily. Despite the shock and pain, I am in quite a good mood. And every now and again my jangled mind flies back to that sleek and shiny forearm and the voice from far above me: 'Have you had a good day?' For some reason this utterly banal line has wormed its way into my quick (or what is left of it). As I am wheeled into a vast, whirring machine – *whir, CLANK, 'Hold still!', CLANK, wheeze* – it strikes me that I . . . but no, I can't hold the thought . . . *thrum, buzz, CLANK* . . . it strikes me that . . . What? I'm in a lift now, I'm whooshing up into the sky. I zoom past a twisted Jesus nailed to the wall, looking pretty much the way I feel. I come to rest. Soft voices fade into the distance. A rubbery silence cocoons me. At last I'm alone in the dark.

This sudden hush, this enveloping dark, is doubly eerie because just two days ago, feeling I should finish it before leaving for Sydney, I hurried to write the final lines of a talk I am to give in Canberra – not next week or even next month, but in the spring. Yet I felt impelled to finish it two days ago. And I decided to call it 'Pushing Against the Dark'. It's about 'lighting a flare' when I write, in order (I think this is what I said) to bring hidden things

But why was I doing that? . . . Who cared about my hidden selves? To be honest, I was actually casting another kind of light. Through language, the only torch I have. In E.M. Forster's phrase about Virginia Woolf's language, I was 'pushing against the dark' – not just the dark that certain hidden selves were crouched in, but a more powerful dark, the dark that, as we grow older, we all feel stealing over us, blotting out inch by inch

what we have loved and who we have been – the dark my gleaming spirals circle around, the emptiness I swirl around, spinning tales. The act of writing is an act of resistance against the mortal condition – not mortality, but the mortal condition . . . in the sense of deepening and magnifying the lived moment while writing. Every syllable I coax from my mind is a push against the dark, a small beam of light that dares the dark to snuff it out. I write to stave off time, to stave off nothingness . . .
'Pushing Against the Dark'

out into the light (hidden selves, for instance, my raw or quirky sides, the facets I know some will mock, the unhealed wounds). By the end of the talk it's clear that I'm really pushing against a much more all-enveloping dark: I write to stave off time, to stave off nothingness. It's as if deep down some part of me knew . . . But no, that's daft, that's superstitious nonsense.

Beyond the window, far away, knifing up out of the blackness, there is a wall of radiance: the city. A nurse comes in with a swish. 'Are you Polish?' I ask, wheezing wetly. 'No,' she says and with another swish she is gone. Russian, I think to myself. What else could she be? She said 'no' in English, but I know she meant '*nyet*'. If she is indeed Russian, given my predilections and the life I've led, it's another tiny coincidence poking out its tongue at randomness. It's any sense of randomness that saps the spirit. Randomness *is* terrifying. Anything but that.

What was it, though, that I was trying to hold onto down there in Emergency? Whatever it was, it's now lying in tangled skeins across my mind. Like me, it has unravelled.

2

Monday

For the rest of the night and the muffled day that follows, I lie staring at the ceiling, or asleep, straining to hear Peter's voice in the unseen corridor outside my room, the voice I've heard every day for half my life. It's strong like sculpted willow. I want every voice I hear to turn out to be his.

Above all he is a voice to me. In thirty years I don't think he's written me a proper letter even once – perhaps an email or two when I've been travelling, a few Post-it notes stuck on the kitchen bench (HAVE FED DOG BACK AROUND 6), but never a letter because we're

9

either just a room away or else we ring. Wherever I am (at the edge of the Sahara, in Vladivostok, Uruguay, Aleppo, or Himachal Pradesh) I find a telephone and call him. I love the way he chuckles when he first hears it's me. But this time, for the time being, flat on my back attached by little leads called cannulas to a cluster of machines and bottles of strange liquids, I can't ring him. Apart from anything else, he has no phone.

Where is he? Did they find him on his ferry? Is he coming? Is he coming soon? Will he fly? He never flies. Flying (for him) is out of the question. Just this once, perhaps? And so I listen. For the rest of the night and the day that follows, I listen, but he doesn't come. Now and again a face peers down at me, a needle goes into my arm, sometimes little groups of people cluster around the bed and stare at me, but mostly I just lie here, muttering to myself in Russian. I even say in impeccable Russian to the nurse who isn't Polish, 'I have soiled myself.' She shows no surprise whatsoever. Where have I dredged up the word for this commonplace of hospital life from? This is not a word I have ever needed, yet up it pops out of some vast sea of Russian words I bob about upon. Lying here on my back I have marvellously shallow thoughts, too. Whole sparkling showers of them billow constantly through my mind.

At some point late on the first afternoon two faces with a bunch of flowers appear from the wings. First

I catch the faint but promising *pock-pock-pock* of sturdy shoes on padded lino and then there they are, two smiling splodges, beside my bed: Karen, who is Russian (sort of) and has organised the reading of my play at NIDA, playing a leading role or two in it, and Anthony, the director, a man I've never met, fiftyish, looking like a slightly weathered imp. I like weathered imps. I squint up at them. If it hadn't been for these two people, in all probability I'd have died in bed alone at home in Hobart, thinking I just had bad indigestion.

'How frightened you must have been!' Karen says, looking a little shaken herself. 'No,' I say, or I think I say, 'I wasn't frightened at all.' They look a little nonplussed at that, even faintly disappointed. It's painful, confronting and somehow outlandish, I'd like to explain to them, but not really frightening. In Michel Houellebecq's novel *Whatever*, which I found myself reading in the plane on the way to Sydney (in another startling coincidence), the nauseating hero also collapses around midnight in the street in a city far from home with pain descending from the shoulders to the chest, is forced, as I was, to ask passers-by for help, ends up like me in a cardiology ward, and is also asked if he felt scared. In order not to make a fuss, he says yes, he did, but admits to the reader that he actually wasn't scared at all. He just had the feeling that he was going to 'cark it' in the next few minutes. 'That's different,' he says.

11

Exactement! Coincidences, I think to myself foggily, can be so vivifying.

They murmur at me for a while, these two visiting apparitions (both beaming, nodding), they're saying something about . . . But really, I have no idea what they're talking about. Probably how the first day's rehearsal of the play has gone. I feel pleased, deeply pleased, almost disproportionately pleased that they're both here by my side, trying to lasso me with words, whole looping strings of them, and tug me back from where I've been floating off to, back towards the light and warmth, and so I wheeze at them through my mask and flap my cannulas at them ('Strictly speaking, cannulae,' I gasp, a pedant to the bitter end). They smile and nod some more, chuckling a bit at the breathless jokes I try to crack, and then squelch back into the wings I can't see into from where I'm tethered.

Silence. How theatrical. In the theatrical silence I wonder briefly what will happen to my play and if I'll ever see it.

In the west, behind the wall of glass beside me, the sky turns green, then indigo, and finally black, and July's sliver of a young moon reappears, immortal, fleetingly, after feigning death, before sliding away into hiding again.

I sleep.

3

Tuesday

It's almost midday before I hear the sound I've been living for, day and night: Peter's voice outside my room. 'In here? Can I go straight in?' And here he is: tall and embarrassed and shaken and brimming over with happiness, pink with winter cold and smiling so much he can hardly speak. Here he is. For the moment I'm still zigzagging around like a damaged kite in a squall, but I know he'll reel me back in.

And he does. With the smell of beef lasagne and grilled fish from distant trays wafting around us (in here it's NIL BY MOUTH, in here to have a sip of water is to flirt with death), he does. In just a few moments I'm back on earth – spreadeagled under the covers, unable to budge, unable to mumble more than a few syllables under my mask, but back.

Yesterday morning, it turns out, on docking in Port Melbourne after a nightmarish crossing of Bass Strait (the roughest in fifty years, they said, so he spent the night vomiting into the toilet-bowl), he drove to his hotel to be told, even before he had time to stagger to the lift, that there was a message for him to tele-phone St Vincent's Hospital in Sydney. Things, he was told when he got through (I can only begin to sense his devastation), 'are not looking good'. (Nobody has yet told me how things are looking. I know they all wish I'd stop bleeding – that's all. And bleeding and bleeding. Allergic to the medication they gave me, I'm filling up with blood. I struggle to sit up a bit from time to time, afraid I might otherwise drown in it. I am shitting blood.) And so he spent all yesterday arranging to fly to Sydney. Flying for him is even more terrifying than crossing Bass Strait in the fiercest storm for fifty years. Yet here he is. He's flown. He laughs. I gurgle. It's as if we were both almost freakishly ill-starred on Sunday evening, practically Bollywood-ishly, catching the eye of some hideous, howling god or goddess of destruction – blue-faced, four-armed Kali, perhaps, brandishing a sword and hung about with severed heads, blood-crazed, yet fiendishly craving more, craving ours. I try to say 'Bloody Kali!' but can't.

Or else, given the way things have panned out, you could say that I (at least) must have an angel keeping watch over me – it depends how you look at these things. 'Someone up there must be keeping an eye on you,' one of the nurses said yesterday. Someone of a Hindu cast of mind might indeed see the hand, not of Kali, but of Ganesh in it (he has four). After all, lying on the pavement in my own filth the night before last, amongst the cigarette butts and streaks of vomit, I could easily have been taken for a disgusting old drunk and been left to die – it's that sort of street, after all. Yet unaccountably I was scooped up by a Good Samaritan – a spikey-haired young Chinese man in a t-shirt with FUCK YOU emblazoned on it, who didn't even tell me his name. (Why did he help me? Why, like all the others, did he not just pass by? In his place, I could well have.) And then, once he had got me back to the hotel, the night porter hesitated, the key to my room in his hand, wondering what to do. Although none of us knew it, my life was in the balance at that moment: if the porter had handed me that key, I'd have gone up to my room and been found dead on my bed by the maid the next morning. Instead he called an ambulance. And the ambulance arrived in minutes and whisked me off to where I could be instantly paddled back to life when I gave up the ghost – as I did, twice.

The gleaming, blond-haired forearm . . . 'Have you had a good day?' It's coming back to me.

'Ill-starred on Sunday evening', 'an angel keeping watch' . . . all this is clearly no more than picturesque gobbledygook. I would like to discuss it with Peter – who is still pink and so intensely alive that I can't stop gazing at him – but just at the moment I can't, so I simply smile crookedly. My eyes are drinking him in. He wouldn't have a bar of either stars or angels. And he's right, of course: at a cosmic level even words such as 'Sunday' are meaningless, let alone 'ill-starred'.

Be that as it may, it has been after lunch on a Sunday that almost anything of any significance to happen to me has happened, ever since I was born – admittedly on a Thursday. I made my unwelcome appearance at Crown Street Women's Hospital on a Thursday morning, just over the brow of the hill from where I am now lying. Ever since then, though, it's been Sunday afternoons and evenings all the way down the line: my mother stopped breathing forever on a Sunday afternoon as I sat beside her bed in the asylum; I first met my wife on a Sunday evening at a friend's house – and she also left me (with no warning at all, I might add) on a Sunday afternoon; my dizzying, transporting encounters with God – not Jesus of Nazareth, I hasten to add,

16

not the Christian sky-god, not the Word made flesh, but the flesh made word, I AM THAT I AM – began on a Sunday, although admittedly that was in the morning, and lasted for years; and I met Peter just after midday on a Sunday several decades ago further along this very street, Peter who turned the rather run-down, sordid world I can't quite see below this window (I'm too high up) into an enchanted realm.

On other, later Sunday evenings, week after week, year after year, in the late 1980s, I recorded my Sunday-night book programme for national radio just over there, where the Harry Seidler building now slices up into the sky in its queer, twisted way, looking out of place and over-dressed in this still oddly dowdy, if expensive, still unsmartened, if forever primping, quarter. At the time Seidler built it, Darlinghurst thought itself on the verge of turning into something stylish, but never did, just like a whore who wakes up each morning swearing she'll never drink cheap liquor again or undersell herself to badly dressed slobs from the wrong suburbs, but always does. From the first one to the last, my programmes all went to air late on a Sunday evening.

Then, at the end of the 1980s, I moved to Melbourne on a Sunday afternoon to make them there and start afresh, coming back to Sydney every few weeks for a while to talk endlessly to my mother – the woman who gave birth to me, whom I'd just met – in the old Top of the Town hotel, here on this very street, a hop, step and a jump away, next to the fire station, also on Sunday afternoons, to find out who I was and who she was and if any of it mattered.

And now *this*. In other words, while things do happen to me on other days in the week (although rarely on a Tuesday), I seem to come to forks in the road on a Sunday after lunch.

For that matter, apropos of Kali, it was on a Sunday afternoon not so long ago that I first came face to face with her, too – in Kuala Lumpur, ironically enough, given that she is an avatar of Brahman, the Cosmic Breath. In Kuala Lumpur, thanks to the fires in Borneo and Sumatra, the air is often so chokingly filthy that you can scarcely breathe at all, or see much past the end of your nose – not that there's anything much to see in Kuala Lumpur even on a clear day. And while I have little time for deities of any kind, let alone for blood-crazed Indian goddesses with four (or sometimes eight, or even ten or twelve or sixteen) arms, the experience was, I must admit, both bizarre and moving. Uplifting? No, not exactly.

What was I doing there? At this precise moment I can't quite remember. My mind is porridge. It will come back to me. I certainly wasn't on a pilgrimage – I have no time for the pilgrimage – but I know it had some-thing to do with Kali.

Peter seems to have gone. I must have drifted off. It's been a long day. Or is it tomorrow?

I lie back in the half-dark, gasping noisily for air. I could do with a bit of the Breath at this very minute, I think to myself, a brush with breathy Brahman. Braaahhman! When I was a teenager I bought a copy of the Upanishads (more for its lurid cover than for its wisdom, I suspect – I was not a seeker after truth by this time, having already found it). I've never forgotten the story of the teacher who is asked by an acolyte how many gods there are. 'Three thousand three hundred and six,' he replies – or some such number.

'Yes, but really how many?' asks the young man.

'Oh, thirty-three, if you insist on knowing.'

'No, but really?'

'Really? Well, really there are six.'

'How many?'

'Three.'

'How many?'

'Two.'

'Not one and a half?'

'Yes, alright, one and a half.'

'No, but *really* how many are there?'

'One.'

'Which one?'

'The Breath. They call him That.'

No doubt from that teacher's point of view I also need to see the One in three thousand three hundred and six – or do I mean the opposite? However, if the truth be told, it's probably a bit late for any of it.

∽

In an idle moment, by the way, once we'd got ourselves home again, I had a look at what the horoscopes had had to say about the day the cosmos unleashed its wrath upon the two of us. Just for fun, you understand, in the spirit of free inquiry. I thought: why not have a quick look? Could be a hoot.

No MENE MENE, TEKEL U-PHARSIN appeared on the dining-room wall the night before – no surprises there, I'm hardly Balthazar, that would have been right out of my class. However, some kind of alert in the local newspaper would not have been too much to ask for, surely, if there really were something to all this fortune-telling business. And by the way, since Balthazar's name has come up, when it comes to astrology, the Babylonians have got a lot to answer for: they were the ones who dreamt the whole thing up in the first place. It is the Babylonian obsession with the number twelve that has left us, thousands of years later, with twelve signs of the zodiac, rather than nine or twenty-three.

If there had been the slightest truth to any of this, given how things panned out, you'd have thought that there'd be at least some vaguely worded tip-off that there was trouble brewing: I wasn't asking for anything spookily specific ('Cardiovascular problems possible around midnight' or 'Ferocious winds and mountainous seas will make a nightmare of any journey northwards across water'), just some hint of the avalanche of misery heading our way, some subtly worded cautionary sign.

Nothing, as it turned out. Not a syllable. And no correction the following day, either, which was odd given how staggeringly off-beam the predictions had been on the Sunday morning. Nuptials – that's all either of us scored in our horoscopes: 'Talk of a wedding', 'You will spend much of today making arrangements to attend an upcoming wedding.' Now, I haven't attended a wedding or given a moment's thought to one since I went to my own more than forty years ago. Who is concocting this drivel?

It's obviously someone who's in it for a bit of a laugh: 'Uranus in your angle of love this week, causing pleasurable vibrations,' 'Time to indulge number one for a change – grab a hottie, lie back and let someone else take charge' – that sort of thing. (These are actual quotes from our local stargazer's offerings.) What sort of fools do they take us for? And why, for that matter, do I read these squirts of hogwash almost every day? What makes them such compelling reading?

4

Wednesday

I'm almost never alone in this white room, except at night. And even at night there's Larissa. She is indeed Russian, it turns out, just as I thought – this nurse who declared she wasn't Polish – and her name is Larissa. From Odessa. Another satisfying swipe at randomness: Odessa figures quite prominently in this play of mine, set as it is in Russia. (Odessa isn't in Russia, strictly speaking, but it might as well be.)

Not that I am Russian, I hasten to add, any more than a man is his wife. More Russian than Chinese, that goes without saying, nobody could be less Chinese than I am, but not at all Russian. Yet I love my idea of Russia (not the real Russia), the small pocket of Russia, still faintly smelling of tsars and Turgenev, that I got to know when I was very young; and I also love every syllable, every phoneme in the overflowing treasure-house that is the Russian language. I love its tumult and its order, its play with infinite disguises, the theatre of it, the whip-cracking three-ringed-circusness of it, its balletic perfection and peacock elegance alongside its earthiness, its sibilance, its oo's and aw's and cascades of syllables. How sad I feel when I admit to myself (as I must, if I'm honest) that I will never know it as I'd like to. I'll never know it, for all my love of it, as intimately as even some ten-year-old street kid in Vladivostok knows it. Yet it's woven into my soul, it's the weft to the warp I was born with. (Since we're talking about Russian, I'll permit myself 'soul'.) I started weaving it in as a small boy – my first two Russian words, as it happens, were *botanicheskiy sad* ('botanical garden'), which I'd found on a Soviet stamp in my shoebox of foreign stamps – and even now, a whole lifetime later, I'm still weaving – very slowly now, and not so deftly, but I come back to the loom from time to time. All the same, I am not in the slightest bit Russian – well, possibly just a touch in my aesthetic responses, but that's the limit of it.

Now we've established that she's Russian, just as I thought, every hour on the hour all night Larissa swishes into my room and asks me in Russian, 'With whom are you conversing?' *S kem vy razgovarivay-ete?* She's just making sure I haven't died again. 'With Larissa,' I answer hoarsely. *S Larissoi.* 'Correct!' she retorts, briskly trilling the 'r' in the Russian word in approval, as if I've just amazed her by accurately calculating pi to the fourteenth decimal point. Then she sails out of the room into that mysterious, softly lit domain everyone comes and goes from, a place of faintly heard voices and quick footsteps, sometimes laughter, a place I can't see and can scarcely picture, where people are fully and unconcernedly alive.

I lie here in the dark each time, chewing over possibilities for 'sailed out of the room' in Russian. Of all the things I might give my mind to as I lie here simultaneously filling up with blood and fighting off pneumonia, not to mention the cardiovascular situation, I give it to how to say 'sailed out of the room' in Russian. (*Vyneslas iz komnaty*? *Vyplyla*? Either?) Does this hint at a kind of basic shallowness in me, or a lightness of spirit that is keeping me afloat? I talk to myself in Russian quite a lot alone in the darkness – I'm not sure why. Perhaps by naming things in a foreign language I am holding everything at one remove, recasting it all as theatre. Perhaps to talk to myself in English would make this nightmare feel all too confrontingly like real life.

Early in the morning, well before first light, even before the Peruvian nurse with the continuous eyebrow comes to take blood, young medical students with exotic names (Mohammed this and Mukesh that), always wearing beautiful silk ties and smiling nervously, start appearing at my bedside to inquire if they might make a time to ask me some questions. 'I hear,' they all begin with a shy smile, 'that you are a very interesting case.' From whom, exactly? In what way 'interesting'? I'm certainly chatty, in a breathless, rather rambling kind of way, if that's what they mean by 'interesting', although I suspect they might mean something more alarming. The Chinese are even more polite than the Indians and Pakistanis, if that is possible. There are so many of these requests that I practically need a social secretary to avoid double-booking.

This morning when I first awake, a whole group of elegantly dressed young people are lined up against the window beside my bed – like pall-bearers, I can't help thinking, waiting for the coffin to be nailed shut. Well, *bonjour à tous!* I croak – at least, I think I do. A *soigné* older man in a suit – possibly the surgeon who saved my life, but I'm not good with faces – is holding forth. They ask me delicate questions. I reply with a disarming frankness. They giggle. They confabulate. They leave. I do enjoy the theatre of these visits, but it's utterly exhausting. I drift off again. The room smells of distant breakfasts and lavender and winter roses.

Later, when the glass towers to the west burst into flame against the cobalt sky, there's first of all a flurry of small, quite unpleasant procedures. Then this morning, excitingly, there's tea. Shortly afterwards a strikingly handsome man in a white coat (square-jawed, trimly bearded) tells me that in his opinion I need a certain operation – 'pronto', as he puts it – but that in the opinion of his white-coated colleague, who is observing me from the end of my bed, it would kill me. At this his colleague smiles wanly. I'm not particularly fussed, to be honest, I'm not afraid, but I do soil myself again.

Not long afterwards, Peter arrives, all rugged up in blue and looking tall, to sit with me in the chair by the window. There is no news. All we can do for the moment is exchange presences. Spreadeagled, I drift off. I am blissfully happy. If I could turn over, I'd be downright ecstatic.

Then I have a visitor (Peter's not a visitor). It's Scott, whom I haven't seen since the Indian disaster. He's talking quietly with Peter and looking rattled. He doesn't quite know what to say when he notices me awake. What is there to say? There's nothing to say. With intimate friends, it's being there together *despite everything* that matters. They face down the Angel of Death for you. They go some miles with you on your journey, that's what they do. 'Bloody Kali!' he says with a stab at levity. I chuckle chestily. Ah, yes, Scott and I know all too well the sort of tricks that vengeful Hindu goddesses can get up to when they're roused.

It was just over there near the Opera House, which I can see glinting in the sunlight, that we met – on a Sunday, as a matter of fact, but that's irrelevant. I'd been casting around for something to do to fill in the day – Sydneysiders, like New Yorkers, tend to believe that their city is brimming over with things to do, but I often find myself stumped to come up with anything at all to do in Sydney that would be transforming, once I've seen the blockbuster from overseas. Eventually I lit upon a Juan Davila exhibition that had just opened at the Museum of Contemporary Art. There's nothing I relish more than seeing highly acclaimed bad art on public display. Bad art in a museum (as opposed to a friend's living room or a cheap motel) is not just a scandal, but positively bracing. It's a clarion call to stand up for what's good and right. So off I set for the museum.

At the top of the echoing staircase, selling tickets to the Davila, sat a Puck, a faintly Sicilian-looking Puck, poised, on the verge of unkempt, but stylishly, almost painstakingly so. You have to be young to get away with it, of course – once you're over twenty-eight you just look scruffy. There's something about the puckish and even the knavish on occasion (not that Scott was that)

that appeals to me. Who better than the trickster to get the old fogey and the mischief-maker inside you firing off each other? We chatted for a while between customers (there weren't many at that hour) about books and art and life, then I tore through the Davila, uttering, as I made to leave, the oldest cliché in the book: 'What time do you finish work?' (I look across at Scott now, a silhouette chatting in a hushed voice to Peter's silhouette, and can't believe I really came out with that line.) 'I know who you are, by the way,' he said quite softly as I headed for the stairs. *Who am I?* When I turned round to see what he might have meant by this, he wasn't even looking at me. He probably dallied in his dark-eyed way with every second customer. The red mist of affection (to quote that wily holy man in *Kim* – an irritating man – what on earth was his name? – who felt even his own affection for Kim to be a sin) was beginning to swirl. I disappeared down the staircase into its billows.

Not long after sunset, to my surprise, he turned up wearing a dandy little hat. Did this mean he was an innocent or a trollop? Can you be both? We went to a café opposite St John's Church, just up the street from where I am lying now – if I could stand up I could see its spire poking up, I'm sure, amongst the down-at-heel blocks of flats and boutique hotels – and I said, with my eye mostly on his waggish little hat, 'I'm off to Tunisia shortly. Would you like to come along?'

(Big decisions like this should be made on the spot, I believe – marriage, moving interstate, even murder, some would say, anything life-changing. Only trivial decisions such as what colour to paint the bathroom should be debated endlessly and looked at from every angle.) 'Yes,' he said, 'I would.' So we went. We met up in a hotel in Tunis, flew to the Sahara and then trundled around the country in crowded buses, our eyes full of electric blues and blinding whites and ornate doors and iron arabesques on windows. Peter, who stayed at home with the ageing German shepherd, didn't seem to much mind – it wasn't an affair, after all: there was to be no monkey business, that was clear from the start, it was hardly even an infatuation, more an enchantment, a friendship with traces of a crush around the edges, and anyway Peter doesn't fly. I am very attracted to people who have not reached their full potential.

All things considered, the trip went well. So not very long ago, with Kali on my mind, I suggested we try India. 'I'm off to Rajasthan shortly,' I said. 'Would you like to come along?' 'Yes,' he said, 'I would.' So we went. We didn't fly off together, I like to leave home alone, but we linked up in Paris – Scott's such a Francophile – and set off for Morocco and then India from there.

Now, in my case there's usually a kind of Shinto side to travel. Although I know almost nothing about Shinto, having visited no more than a handful of Shinto

30

shrines in Kyoto, I do know that worshippers walk to the shrine – and I can feel a pleasurable excitement stirring in my limbs at the mere thought of this – along an approach road called a *sandō*, whose beginning is marked with a sacred wooden gateway (a *torii* of some description – often bright vermillion). These days in Japan the *sandō* may start a long way from the shrine itself amidst a jumble of crowded shops. That's where you pass through the gate on your way to the sanctuary, that's where the experience of self-renewal begins, surrounded, anciently, by sideshows, tournaments and buffoonery. And so it is with me – and travel *is* a festival with me, a rite, an annual cleansing ritual, a ceremony of rebirth, a precious time of dressing-up and spells and following paths through 'straightened nature' (as the Japanese call it – rarely wildness). I'm not talking about flights on budget airlines to visit friends, or trips to carry out some task (like this one to Sydney), but my annual journey in search of . . . (goodness me, I nearly said 'spiritual') . . . restoration. I travel to restore something – a sense of being my own master, perhaps (you're never your own master at home, time is at its most oppressive at home), or leisure in its purest form. My *torii* is my own green front door. That's where my *sandō* begins, that's where I start to abandon reason (and how painful that is) for intuition, and intellect for feeling, so that for a season, just a short season, I might see with the heart. Closing my front door and turning round to face the world from my verandah is a moment of voluptuous excitement.

My first stop for a spot of purification on the way to Rajasthan was Kuala Lumpur – an odd choice at first glance. Nowhere on Earth could be less like one of those sacred waterfalls that the Japanese like to stand under on their way to the shrine to cleanse themselves of impurities – well, more than that: to violently wash away who they've been at home since last time. But then it's all just symbolic, really, isn't it, and, rightly framed, symbols can be potent anywhere.

I wanted to arrive in Rajasthan, my final destination, ready for what I'd see. I didn't want to just stand about at the back of a temple or two, watching devotees perform their outlandish rituals as I might in some cathedral in France. Nor did I want to join in, though. Taking part in ceremonies I don't believe in, even attending weddings or Christmas dinners, embarrasses me. I never worship or adore. I should try to be more relaxed about it, I know, but worship makes me feel a fraud.

You have to strike a balance, especially in India: open and curious, but not about to go native. Thousands of Westerners go native every day all over the country, often out-chanting and out-gyrating the locals in their new-found fervour and ballooning costumes. Nobody tries to go native in Japan, for instance, barely even in Mexico – not *native*, not really. But for some reason India is awash with comfortably-off Westerners decked out in crumpled dhotis and shalwar kameezes like down-and-out Bollywood extras, ecstatically pretending to be what they patently are not. Going native all-together, it was called sneeringly at St Xavier's in Lucknow, according to Kipling. It's demeaning to everybody, the boys are told, to pretend that one is not a sahib when one clearly is. Yet it still goes on. The wealthier the foreigner, the more extravagant the display. It was in McLeod Ganj in the Himalayan foothills, where the Dalai Lama has his compound, that I saw the most discomfiting examples: middle-aged women with Alice in Wonderland hair from Melbourne and Milwaukee mooning about in search of the spiritual moment that will last a lifetime (to misquote Casanova) – a few men in crushed linen pants and no socks, swathed in scarves, but mostly women. You'll bump into them all over India, not just in Himachal Pradesh, but particularly where the landscape seems either inspiringly elevated or forgiving – along the dreamy lakeshore in Udaipur, for instance, or on the beach in Goa. What *is* the attraction of Indian religions for Westerners? What is it that casts the spell? It's got something to do with the way they can claim not to be *religions*, as such, I suspect. 'Oh, it's not a religion, it's a way of life' – how many times have I heard that?

What I wanted on that trip was not Enlightenment, in which I do not, of course, believe, but enlightenment. Kali, I remember now, seemed to offer a promising, and for me quite novel, approach to it. Yes, since I've been rather caught up in recent years with the question of how to think about time, Kali, goddess of Time and Change, promised to concentrate the mind very nicely. (And that's what you want when you travel: to condense, to crystallise anew, in the chaos that your daily life has turned into.) Is that, perhaps, what Kali really *is*, with all those arms of hers, that blue skin, that necklace of skulls, the bloody scimitar and her murderous leer: one of the faces of time, what you see when you focus your mind on the destructive side to time's unfolding? (And that's what I feel besieged by.) Not you or I, of course, no eight-armed, blood-sucking goddess revelling in hecatombs of gushing slaughter is going to come naturally into *our* minds – at least, not traditionally – when we ponder time. But in India things have always been different.

To prepare myself for Rajasthan, I wanted to come into Kali's presence (as it were) with a devotee who would be sensitive to my very Western inner world. In Kuala Lumpur I happen to know someone who fits the bill perfectly: someone almost more Western than I am, and certainly better educated, yet an ardent worshipper of Shiva's ferocious consort – 'consumed by Kali

34

passion', as he puts it, claimed as a 'Son of Kali'. In other words, in terms of religion, someone schooled in things I've never had much time for at all. His name is Prakash.

When I rang Prakash to sound him out, he was bemused, but said he'd be pleased to take me to his 'little temple'. 'Do stop over,' he said. 'We'll start a wonderful conversation.' And he emailed me a poem about the goddess.

It didn't go quite as I'd imagined it would, this first encounter with Time Itself. I did feel intensely enlivened, as I think I wrote in my diary, but it was not a waterfall along the way, or not, at least, my idea of one. What I'm most susceptible to if I am to be catapulted into another kind of awareness is the merging of a particular kind of sumptuousness with a soaring lightness, found, as the English writer Adam Nicolson once remarked, in certain English churches and almost nowhere else. There was none of that sumptuousness or lightness here. Yet I *was* moved.

'What's that?' Scott asks, leaning closer. Peter puts down his book to listen.

Did I just speak? 'Moved,' I shlumpfle. 'I *was* moved.'

'Moved?'

'Yes.'

'Moved where?'

Oh, never mind.

I lie utterly still like a pile of sticks under the covers, yet inside my mind is somersaulting wildly. I am nowhere, I am everywhere. I am forgetting, I am remembering. Vividly.

5

I am swooning in a haze of sweetness, a troubling, scented sweetness, I do not want to be here, yet my being seems to have congealed here, there's a fixedness to my stare as the priestess rotates her camphor candle before the goddess in this tiny temple, this gleaming candlelit box of a temple stuffed with idols, there's hardly room in it for Prakash, his priestess and me along with the garish idols, I do not want to be here, I do not like the sweetness, I think of cobras swaying to the thin, sweet sound of a flute, it is not a loving sweetness, I cannot breathe. And then it doesn't matter that I cannot breathe. I am so small now that I no longer need to breathe. I am infinitesimally small, a speck of nothing. And then she reaches out, this grey-garbed priestess, this unadorned old woman draped in grey, and lightly touches me between my eyebrows, so now I have a bright red bindi on my forehead, slightly skew-whiff and smudged, but turning my mind into an exclamation mark (unexpectedly), and I am vivified, and now both large and small and also neither all at once, immense, the size of Saturn, and also smaller than a pinhead, here in Kuala Lumpur, in Brickfields, to be precise, somewhere I would never want to be, in the lurid religious bazaar of Brickfields, there's hardly room for the shops and houses amidst all these gaudy places of worship, I'm feeling queasy, if the truth be told, from all this scented worshipping . . .

Here my notes from my third day in Kuala Lumpur trail off. Perhaps it's just as well: I was clearly getting overwrought.

∽

Is this what it felt like to wander through Ephesus or Corinth two thousand years ago? In Brickfields, somewhere in the sprawling chaos of Kuala Lumpur, there's a shrine to a different god on every corner. Not completely sure of where I was going, I jumped out of the taxi in front of Our Lady of Fatima, which is just past the vast Buddhist Maha Vihara compound next door to the Zion Evangelical Lutheran cathedral, not so very far from the Tamil Methodist church and St Mary's Orthodox Syrian Cathedral, not to mention the jolly Brickfields Ganesh temple, noisiest and most colourful house of worship of the lot. It was Saturday night and I was indulging in a practice Kali run with a friend of a friend of a friend before meeting up with Prakash on the Sunday.

The friend of a friend of a friend was a formidably self-possessed Indian woman whose private pantheon, as it turned out, crammed into a small taper-lit room just off the kitchen in her flat, included Jesus, Buddha, a quite dazzling array of Hindu gods and goddesses, as well as a copy of the Koran, just to be on the safe side. The Hare Krishna theme song was playing softly in one corner. I'd never encountered this kind of religious promiscuity before. Indifference, certainly – wherever you have multiculturalism, you have indifference – but not this kind of religious profligacy in one woman. What on earth inspires it? A blanket misunderstanding of what any of these creeds teaches? A sort of bob-each-way, lucky-dip approach to truth? A naïve attempt to appear tolerant in a deeply intolerant society? After all, if, for instance, Jesus got it more or less right, or if Muhammad did, then a lot of what all the others had to say was hogwash. Before I'd had a chance to inquire, however, my friend's friend's friend had whisked me down into the dogma-drenched streets of Brickfields in the smog below her apartment. After a brisk walk in the muggy, malodorous heat, we came to the door of a shed where we were greeted with a notice that read: PIPE WASH HAND AND LEG. Our extremities duly dampened, in we went.

Now, I hadn't been expecting the Great Mosque of Damascus, let alone Chartres Cathedral – let me make that quite clear from the start. I suppose what I'd had in mind was something plain, along the lines of a Quaker meeting house, say, but with rather more idols and smells than most Quakers would feel comfortable with (although I find Quakers unnaturally comfortable with almost anything, which makes them impossible to argue with, as Voltaire observed) and a spotlit Kali, all flailing arms and severed heads, snarling at us in one corner. What I hadn't imagined was a drafty suburban outhouse with a few plastic statues lining the walls: Jesus, Mary, Buddha, Ganesh and quite a choice of Kalis, including one holding up the iconic severed head. It felt as if I'd stumbled into the backyard lean-to of some crazed religious fetishist. (Which is an ungracious way of describing what it probably was: the shed Tamil railway workers had fitted out as a shrine to their goddess decades ago when Brickfields was a squatter enclave.) Two dogs lay tethered in moody silence against one wall, while a few roosters strutted in and out, looking bored to death. A depressed-looking woman was mopping the floor. Nobody else was there. I felt nothing more than if I'd been staring at a side-show in a theme park. I did not feel that my companion had any deep affection for this place, either, despite her openness to every creed, or that the woman mopping the floor was mopping out of love for it, or from any other passion.

At the small, fragrant Ganesh temple a few streets away the scene was much livelier, I must say, with worshippers prostrating themselves before their brightly lit, garlanded idols. Yet I still felt little joy in being there, no real upwelling of rarefied feelings in the camphor-laden air, no hint of what I can only call *spirit* – in which I do not believe, although I am willing to be ambushed by it if it exists. (Transcendence is a completely different matter: I've always got my eye out for transcendence. I caught no glimpse of it here, though. Perhaps transcendence is not on offer in suburban Ganesh temples.)

Eventually I took the monorail back to the city centre, feeling slightly disenchanted – definitely untransported – and, to be honest, a little apprehensive of what I might experience the next day when I was to go with my friend Prakash to *his* Kali temple to watch him worship. According to Prakash, a subtle, Oxford-educated man, a cobra from the field behind his temple slithers in at the full moon to sway before the fearsome snake goddess Manasa, staring at her and she (big-eyed, bad-tempered, swathed in red and gold) at him. Perhaps there, the next day, with any luck I would feel . . . how can I explain it? . . . not just transported, but *looked at in the eye* from beyond all this. That's what you want: to feel looked at, not as Christians tend to think of it (God peering down at them ceaselessly, counting the hairs on their heads and so on), but in a sudden, interlocking way. Eyeballed, but in a nice way. *Darshan*, in other words: being beholden at the very instant you behold the beholder – or at least the illusion of it – I see but am also seen. Eyes – yes, Hindu temples, come to think of it, are indeed full of marvellous, riveting eyes.

As it turned out, the next day with Prakash everything was very different. Exactly what was different is hard to say. It even began differently, more upliftingly, with a cheering visit to the laneway of flowers just off Jalan Tun Sambanthan back in Brickfields, where we watched our garlands of marigold and rose petals being woven. (I couldn't object to pink and gold garlands; it was a mere politeness – it didn't mean I was 'going native'.) What was really different, though, from the trial run, once we got to the temple, was the vivid sense of Prakash's belief – joyful belief – in a real presence there with us in that pokey little room no

42

bigger than my hotel bathroom, as well as the open-heartedness of his desire to show the Divine Mother (as he calls this capriciously wrathful deity) that he loves her. Or at least that he adores her – honours, reveres and feels a passionate attachment to her.

I'm not sure, by the way, that *love*, devoid of any animality, as an English-speaking Christian might apply this word to the supremely Good, should be looked for in a Kali temple. In a Kali temple you don't expect the omnipresent life-force in the universe to be revealed as *love*. In the Indian imagination, for very good reason, it is much more ferocious. I'm not sure that in a Kali temple you even have the sense you have in the sort of Protestant church I was familiar with as a child that *all will be well*. In a Kali temple, you might look, as many a Christian would in church, for the possibility of God being *in* everything (sort of . . . omnipresent at the very least), but not for the possibility that all will be well. Not really. There's something rather Western, middle-class and sentimental, surely, about thinking of *lovingkindness* as a divine attribute or human virtue. Prakash, for instance, with his Tamil background, sees it as almost a namby-pamby quality. For him, loving-kindness, together with disinterested courtesy and altruism, is a Western luxury born of economic security. He said so over lunch. The Greek gods had no time for mercy or compassion, either: Zeus and his progeny are as stony-hearted as earthquakes and thunderstorms. There wasn't much love in the air on Mount Olympus.

Yet I am addicted to it. 'Though I speak with the tongues of men and of angels,' we read in Sunday School, 'and have not charity, I am become a sounding brass, or a tinkling cymbal. And though I have the gift of prophecy, and understand all mysteries, and all knowledge; and though I have all faith, so that I could remove mountains, and have not charity, I am nothing.' (Paul's First Epistle to the Corinthians – the King James version, obviously. How it sings!) At the end of this luminous lesson in love – and in reflecting the Love that is God – Paul says with what I hear as a soaring, if ungrammatical, gentleness: 'And now abideth faith, hope, charity, these three; but the greatest of these is charity.' (That is, *caritas, agape* – love.) This is really not the sort of thing you're likely to find in the *Bhagavad Gita*.

Brought up in a nice middle-class suburb of Sydney in the 1940s and 50s, a dullish suburb of roomy bungalows and lawns and nice, mild-mannered people, on the notion that, however unlikely it might seem, the source of all being is Love, I still find it hard to warm to any deity who isn't. *Darshan* sounds soul-quickening, but I would like the interlocking gazes to be loving as well. Very lower North Shore, I can see that. It has the ring of something that nice parents in Lane Cove supposedly felt for their children and nice children at Lane Cove

Public School ideally felt for their parents. (What the children at St Michael's Catholic School up the road or their parents felt, it was better not to speculate.) I suspect we confused Christianity with niceness. Was Jesus nice? Not really, when you read between the lines, not in a Lane Cove sense. Yet my life overflowed with niceness. I encountered unhappiness, obviously, as a child, even misery, but not evil. I saw suffering, but never experienced violence or brutality. If I'd been a Tamil migrant worker building the railways in Malaya a century ago, my idea of who was running the universe would understandably have been quite different.

The other source of my genuine transport that afternoon in Prakash's tiny temple was the very ordinariness of the stuffy, tiled chamber itself, with its jars of cleaning fluid stacked under the benches where the gods sat. It was as unremarkable as my next-door neighbour's poultry shed – again, for good reason: this shrine was one of many built where Tamil workers had seen an apparition in the early part of the last century. There was no awe before the Awful, no astonishment at the Astounding, no enactment of paradise to buoy up the soul. (There was wonder, though, I'm told.) Even the priestess, drably dressed, the granddaughter of the founder, moving with her candles from image to image, speaking softly in Tamil to each one, was indistinguishable from any number of other older Indian women you might glimpse working away at some humble task in somebody's kitchen or laundry on your way to the temple. It's easy to soar wonder-struck on waves of bliss in a Gothic cathedral with organ music thundering all around you, but in a dark sanctuary the size of a suburban boxroom, surrounded by plastic statues and bottles of household detergent, for an ecstatic lurch to happen it takes something else.

It was the collision of the suburban and the celestial here that had force. Perhaps it's always some sort of collision – the collision of heaven and earth, say, in many churches – that propels us higher, or leaves us speechless with a kind of spiritual astonishment (although I don't of course trust that slippery word 'spiritual' one little bit). Here it was the collision of unfeigned humbleness on the one hand (my friend called it 'humility', which makes it sound like a practised virtue, but I'd call it 'humbleness') – not the European monk's humbleness, buttressed by the almost unimaginable wealth of the Roman Catholic establishment, but the humbleness of a washerwoman, the lowliness of an almost invisible nobody who can't read or write – with, on the other hand, the conviction that the Divine Mother, Time Itself, had been present with us, coaxed to smile on us (of all the beings in the universe), right there in Brickfields, Malaysia, right then. It was the clash of a finely honed intellect (my friend's) with utter ignorance. It was shabbiness rubbing up against a kind of radiant refinement or . . . oh, there's that word again . . . *spiritual* elegance.

Or was it just an unlettered old lady, a man with goddess delusions and a fatigued tourist bumping into each other in a stuffy, ill-lit shed in Kuala Lumpur? After all, with the right sound effects and lighting, it seems that most of us will believe anything. (Even without sound effects and lighting: within days of arriving home, I watched a British television program showing a roomful of non-believers being hypnotised to fall over backwards and then wake up believing in God – not in Santa Claus, mind you, not in the powers of Persil to wash whiter, but in God. Which they all did: over they went, one after the other, SHLUMPF, SHLUMPF, SHLUMPF, and then back up they came believing in the Jesus-in-the-sky scenario, something not even the hypnotist himself, Derren Brown, believed in.)

To put it bluntly, I'm also not sure that I can trust my own judgement here. When it comes to religion, there's something in the air in Malaysia that strikes me as distinctly on the nose. This country is a hothouse of bizarre blooms, a fecund breeding ground for the outlandish and the daft. Where else but in Malaysia could the Sky Kingdom cult have flourished, for instance? Not even in the United States of America, surely, except possibly in Utah, could you

get a following of thousands for a religion that vener-
ates a gigantic cream-coloured teapot, with matching
two-storey-high blue vase and giant yellow umbrella.
You can't visit this display of divine crockery and
umbrella any more because, a few years ago, after a
fatwa had been slapped on the sect for insulting Islam,
a religion particularly sensitive to any kind of slight
or affront, the teapot, vase and giant parasol were all
smashed to pieces by government decree. The founder,
believed by his followers to be the reincarnation of
Shiva, Buddha, Jesus and Muhammad, has wisely fled
across the nearby border into Thailand to prepare for
his next incarnation as the Imam Mahdi (the messianic
redeemer of Islam, last seen alive in the Sudan in 1885).
What devotees there are left, most having been jailed or
driven underground as apostates, worship angels and
forest fairies as well as God, who is said to pour his
blessings upon mankind from a vast *spiritual* teapot in
the sky. I am not describing events from five hundred
years ago. This is all happening now, as I write these
lines, just a few hours up the road from Kuala Lumpur.

'Do you have any questions for me?' the smiling
priestess asked in Tamil when it was time to go.

'Not today,' I said with a slight catch in my voice.

She smiled again and said nothing.

We left. I did not feel at peace. Pricked awake by
real presences, perhaps, but not at peace – too queasy,

out of place and out of breath for that. Something felt out of kilter as we walked back to the car, something seemed askew. Was I guilty of bad faith? If so, then in India a few weeks later I was to be punished for it with an almost comic theatricality, and poor Scott was caught in the line of fire. Kali is pitiless about this sort of thing.

I somersault back into the ward and land SPLAT, spreadeagled again on my bed. Over against the window Scott is intent on writing something in a notebook, glancing up occasionally to stare at the day outside. Peter must be off getting himself some lunch. Or is it dinner-time already? No, I'd have smelt it. In any case, the sky is not yet pink enough, it's still a cold, unblinking blue. I'd like to talk to him about India, I'd like to speak my heart, but I can't simply snuffle at him from beneath this mask, so I just look and remember. I remember Udaipur (its stench, its splendour); I remember Jodhpur and the cobalt-blue houses of the Brahmins below the fort; I remember Jaipur, the grandeur and the squalor and the Finns in shorts. I remember the controlled hysteria at Kali's temple in the Amber Fort outside the city. I remember the night we tried to leave Jaipur.

6

Despite being moved in Kali's temple in Kuala
Lumpur, I don't believe in her, not literally, or in any
of her black-faced manifestations: Durga Kali, Maa
Shakti, Lord Shiva's wife, Divine Mother, Daughter
of Himalaya (the list seems endless) – none of them.
Honestly, what a lot of gobbledygook! I am no more
tempted to believe in these folk-tales than I am in
the swarm of ancient Greek stories about the godlets
and their vassals inhabiting the forests, seas and
mountains of the eastern Mediterranean two or three
millennia ago.

All the same, the night Scott and I tried to leave India, *some* god or other grew implacable, the heart of *some* being beyond all understanding grew black. With each passing hour the situation became more and more catastrophic. Given where we were (Rajasthan), and the timing (it was the last night of the Navratri festival), it was hard not to ask ourselves if we'd done something to incur Kali's wrath – just in a manner of speaking, of course.

We'd already got ourselves into and out of several sticky situations by the time we came to leave Jaipur for home, as one does when travelling – it's perfectly natural, especially heading towards the equator, and in particular after dark in the medina in Fez. But the situation that unfolded in Jaipur was not just sticky, it was calamitous: it was that strange mixture of the disastrous and the farcical on a grand scale that will always smack of supernatural mischief.

My point is this: as we took off into the night sky above the city, heading for Delhi, at the end of the tenth day of the Durga Puja on which revellers celebrate the Kali's supposedly softer side, or at least her victory over evil, her demon-slaughtering side as opposed to her much darker all-devouring, all-destroying side, and the plane began to heave and judder and then lumber back down towards the fireworks puncturing the blackness beneath, life suddenly started to play out exactly as it would have if Kali had indeed existed. On this, the tenth, night of the waning moon, with the crowds still roistering invisibly amongst the feathery star-bursts of light below us, everything went hideously, almost laughably, askew. Things often do, apparently, when Kali is summoned from Durga's brow (*out she leaps, enraged, swollen tongue bright red and craving blood*) to slay the demons of self-delusion. Before you know it she's simply gone berserk, working herself up into an uncontrollable frenzy of demon-slaughtering, until she is eventually calmed by Shiva (her consort, who is himself god of destruction – that's how bad things can get). To make matters worse, from every drop of blood she spills sprouts yet another demon. Quite spontan-eously, as we wheeled to land back in Jaipur, jolting earthwards across the erupting city, with our landing-gear stuck (down, fortunately, not up), hoping we weren't about to crash-land in a ball of fire, we looked at each other, Scott and I, and said, 'Kali!' You could feel the swish of her sword coming closer, her lust for heads to fly. It was uncanny: after all, she doesn't exist.

Back in the terminal, once we'd scrambled from the plane out onto the tarmac ('Let me off *immediately*,' the Indian passengers had started shouting in rich upper-class British accents after we'd landed, 'I *demand* you open the door and let me disembark!'), there were certainly unslaughtered demons aplenty where before there had been none. You'd tap someone on the shoulder to ask for assistance, someone who just an hour or two earlier had been the very soul of helpfulness, and – POOF! – as if by some black art, when he swivelled to face you, his smile would have turned into a taunting sneer, his eyes now flashing with spite. *'Come back in the morning.'*

'But we'll miss our connection.'

'Move aside, you are hampering me.'

'Hampering?'

'Hampering.'

He'd very likely have a gaggle of wheedling helper goblins buzzing around him, too, pulling at us, baiting us, trying to tempt us into doing things that would lead to our certain and hideous downfall – make a midnight dash up the wreck-strewn highway to Delhi Airport, for instance, *very cheap, special price just for you*, death in a pile of mangled steel almost guaranteed.

There were even more demons waiting for us in Delhi when we finally did get there the next morning on another plane, having indeed missed our connection out of India during the night. There was one particularly aggressive one, for example, standing with a machine-gun at the entrance to the international terminal, refusing point-blank to let us in. 'Your plane has already left,' he snarled gleefully, after a glance at our tickets, 'so your tickets are invalid. And you can't come in without a valid ticket.'

'But that's the whole point, you see: we need to get into the overseas terminal in order to get a valid ticket.'

'Well, you can't. You can only come in with a valid ticket.'

'But, don't you see . . .'

'Move out of the way. You're blocking the entrance.'

'It's Kali,' Scott muttered, despite himself, 'it's bloody Kali!' I doubt he believes in Kali any more than I do (probably less) – the words just came out of their own accord. He opened his mouth and heard himself curse Kali. Where was Ganesh, divine Remover of Obstacles (and Kali's de facto stepson), when you needed him?

Not long after, *mirabile dictu* (as the Romans used to say, knowing a thing or two about marvels), he turned up! Now, Ganesh can be found at the entrance to every Kali shrine – somewhere around the doorway (in a carved frieze, say, or as a stone statue to one side) you'll see his elephant-head and beneficent smile, blessing you as you go in to face whatever it is the goddess has in store for you. However, it turns out that to *really* get things moving with Ganesh you need to chant the mantra *'Om vigneshwaraya namah'* 108 times a day in a state of purity – there's always a catch, isn't there – but we were unaware of this that day. Once he arrived, though, our manifestation of Ganesh – Vikram from the tour agency – made a valiant effort to stem the growing cascade of divine malevolence. Either through sorcery or because he had a special pass, young Vikram (willowy, slim-wristed Vikram, the epitome of grace, not elephantine in appearance at all) eventually succeeded in ushering us into the departures hall past the demon with the machine-gun. We approached the airline counter.

'Ah,' said the swarthy demon manning the desk, scanning our invalid tickets with a frown. 'You need new tickets.'

'Yes, we do.' I'd never seen such blackly gleaming hair in all my life, every single follicle carefully oiled and combed.

'Well, you can't get them here,' he said with the kind of evil delight only Indian and Russian officialdom can muster. By comparison, the rude immigration officials at Heathrow, for instance, are just uncouth amateurs. 'For new tickets you have to go to our office on the third floor.'

'Fine.'

'But you can't go to our office on the third floor without valid tickets.'

'Ah,' I said. Who was scripting this piece of buffoonery? Or was it a tragedy? It was certainly turning into a nightmare. Would it help if I had a seizure? I can do spectacular seizures. Were we to become stateless aliens, eking out the rest of our lives in the departures hall at Delhi Airport, living off the charity of passing strangers?

'Now, move out of the way, please,' he snapped. 'You're holding up the queue.'

I tried to ring the travel agency at home in Australia, well out of Kali's range, surely, to see if they could intervene with the airline. It was closed. Australians are accustomed to the whole country closing down every second Monday, but this was a Thursday. It turned out to be the Thursday of Show Day in Hobart. However, since it *was* a Thursday afternoon during normal office hours, the agency's emergency number was not connected. Hobart was clearly not out of Kali's range at all.

Here in India, Vikram, still doggedly incarnating Ganesh, did eventually manage to get an airline booking clerk in Mumbai on his mobile, but it took him eight hours to make the necessary arrangements. Early on, while reading out ticket numbers to our invisible saviour on the other side of the country, he dropped his phone and broke it. Managing to beg a replacement off a passing colleague, he began all over again. He got hold of another booking clerk, but was soon put on hold. He was put on hold for hours at a time. Finally, the replacement phone ran out of battery power, severing the newly re-established connection with the all-powerful booking clerk in Mumbai. Vikram spent quite a few of the remaining hours bent double at a public recharging point, while at the same time trying to stay on the line to rebook us to Australia. After about three hours hunched over like this, he began to look mad and deformed.

At the last moment, almost a day after the first ominous screeches and lurches on that plane attempting to take off from Jaipur, we were offered tickets home on the last flight for the day. We could have them and make a dash for the departures gate just as soon as we came up with the astronomical sum of money somebody had decided new tickets would cost – several years' salary, probably, for the dapper young man keeping the toilets spick and span at the other end of the hall.

But Kali had not finished with us yet: my bank back in Australia, thinking that we should have left India by now, refused to process my requests for money. ERROR! ERROR! it squawked. The eyes of the airline staff went cold. They looked across the desk at us, snatching up the tickets they'd been on the point of handing over, as if we'd turned out to be criminals. The cosmos was mocking us, clearly – any fool could see that. Some malign cosmic force was zapping us with a concentrated stream of celestial spite, delighting hugely in our torment.

Two revolutions of the earth later, in a state of sweaty dishevelment, staggering with fatigue and looking so beaten and abused that even the airport staff became alarmed, we arrived back in Melbourne. Tireless Ganesh had won. We had not been in a war zone, we had not been caught in a bombing raid or abducted by terrorists, but we *felt* as if we'd been allowed to play in the sun for a while – to blunder about in the palaces and pleasure-gardens of Udaipur, Jodhpur and Jaipur, unmindful of Who was Who and What was What, disrespectful of the resident deities – and then been gleefully swatted. Not crushed to death, but swatted over and over again and then spat upon by some spirit of blackness in the sky (or its consort). That's how it *felt*.

But *had* we been unmindful and disrespectful? There had been one unfortunate incident in the Amber Fort in the hills outside Jaipur, it's true. There, the day before we left, festooned with marigolds, a bindi on my forehead, I had joined the almost hysterically adoring melee at the great silver doors of the fort's Kali temple and gone inside (been virtually sucked inside by the torrent of worshippers) to where the priests were accepting libations of whisky . . . *with a leather wallet still in my pocket*. And no whisky (being a teetotaller myself). I'd left my leather belt outside, as well as my shoes, but not my wallet. Surely an Infinite Spirit, or even just a common and garden Divine Being, would understand my reluctance: after all, it wasn't evensong at All Saints, South Hobart we were trying to gatecrash, it was the last chance before lunch on the particularly holy ninth day of the Navratri festival in Kali's honour for tens of thousands of pilgrims to throng the Shila Devi temple to worship her. In any case, let's not get *too* pernickety about the skins of dead animals affronting the goddess glowering in her alcove: after all, for several centuries a goat was sacrificed here on a daily basis – right up until 1980, as a matter of fact – and it's a pretty safe bet that it was not put to death mercifully. Indeed, for that matter, for centuries Kali was not averse to human sacrifice: the bands of Thugs who terrorised India for five hundred years specialised in the ritualistic killing of travellers in honour of Kali. The wallet in my pocket was surely a very minor misdemeanour, if it was an affront to the goddess.

Everywhere else, though, we had been well-behaved to a fault. (Hadn't we?) In Udaipur, for example, the pastel-coloured city dreaming beside its lakes in southern Rajasthan, we not only went *before doing anything else at all* – even before visiting the famous Lake Pichola or the incomparable city palace on its shores – to the towering Jagdish temple behind our hotel to watch Vishnu, the All-pervading Essence of the Universe in Its most sustaining form (I'm starting to tire of all these ridiculous titles), being deliriously worshipped by a crowd of elderly locals and a sprinkling of overwrought Europeans, while we stood quietly at the back trying very hard to be reverent and open-minded, despite the mayhem, so unlike anything encountered in a house of worship at home where the sacred is more associated with silence; but also, every evening in Udaipur, and then later in Jodhpur, we stood for hours in the pulsating night air, watching the *Raas-Garba* stick dancers slowly circling, barefooted boys clockwise on the outside, barefooted girls anticlockwise on the inside, hundreds of them, perhaps thousands, gaudily dressed in reds and greens and yellows, filling the street beneath the festive lights, clacking each other's sticks to deafening music, twirling sometimes, sometimes not, in an endlessly repeated ritual clacking, like flocks of brilliantly coloured jungle birds mating in front of us, mindlessly, perfectly, blissfully – not, though, exuberantly – rhythmically clacking them, over and over and over they'd CLACK *clap-clap* CLACK *clap-clap* CLACK *clap-clap*, clacking for what felt like hours until . . . WHOOMPF. Silence. For the goddess. For Kali. In joy.

Afterwards, in Udaipur, drifting back down to the lakeside where our hotel stood, through inky-black streets and laneways, we could barely speak. In the silky darkness we felt bathed in light, in the softly breathing silence we felt we'd just been drowned in sound. All of a sudden a lithe figure in white appeared in front of me as if conjured out of thin air. 'Hullo, sir, hullo!' In the shadows on the left there was muffled laughter. 'Hullo, sir, hullo! My friend, sir,' – more boyish laughter from the pitch-black doorway, the dance of glowing cigarettes – 'my friend, sir,' and he nodded at the doorway, 'thinks you look very handsome, sir, like an Indian. He would like to bite you.' And I laughed out loud, and he laughed, and Scott laughed, and in the doorway the tips of the cigarettes zigzagged around like fireflies as the others, too, laughed. As we had seen in countless temple carvings, it was all so seamless for them, as it never can be for us, this dovetailing patchwork of courtship, devotion, godliness, passion, play and erotic sentiment – at least it was supposed to be seamless, at least it could be.

Only at the Shila Devi temple in the Amber Fort, as I say, right at the end, on the point of leaving Jaipur, did I slip up. Only in the aftermath of that particular indiscretion did I begin to feel a hint of black-heartedness in the air. And even then, eventually, as I've related, out of the steamy smog blanketing the airport in Delhi, our own private Ganesh, a figure of grace as Ganesh is supposed to be, arrived to take up position precisely where Ganesh is meant to be found – at the entrance to Kali's domain – to remove the obstacles besetting us. Most Indians will touch Ganesh's head before leaving on a journey. At Delhi airport we did the next best thing: we shook Vikram's hand. Moments later we were sucked up into the sky and disappeared.

As I say, I believe in none of this Kali or Ganesh

business in any literal sense. Not for a split second. All religion, after all, as E. M. Forster put it pithily in *A Passage to India*, is really just a collection of *bons mots*. Which doesn't mean there is nothing left to say after the universe has been described, it just means that religious *bons mots* rarely make a good fist of it. But the funny thing about Hinduism (unlike Christianity and Islam) is that you don't have to believe any of it literally if you don't feel so inclined. Everything you say about the universe, in the final analysis, is just a way of speaking. There's something deeply liberating about the Hindu take on things.

India hit Scott and me like a cloudburst of sensations, colours, faces, bodies and sounds. It washed everything else away – France dissolved, Fez shrank to nothing. It's a maddening, brutal, unforgiving country, the cities well into the evening full of screeching squalor, the countryside exhausted and despairing, yet I can't wait to go back.

'Would you go back to India?' I ask Scott's silhouette.

'Tomorrow,' he says. 'Would you?'

I cackle gluggily. Will there be a tomorrow for me? 'Do you think I'll be able to travel again?' I asked the doctor yesterday as she took my wrist. (She's Zimbabwean, I think. I can't remember ever seeing anybody quite so flawlessly beautiful at such close quarters before in all my life.) 'First let's get you out of here alive,' she said briskly. Fair enough. I decided to leave it at that for the moment.

But yes, I would, I'd go back 'tomorrow'. Why? All I can think to tell myself is what the writer Donald Richie says when asked why he lives in Japan: 'I like myself there.' Curiously, I didn't much like myself in Austria or Brazil, for example, where millions find themselves very interesting indeed, but I do like myself in India. As soon as I arrive, my psyche's deepest roots are galvanised. For a season I thrive in the controlled hysteria of the streets, bazaars and temples. For the next year or two, the shrine at the end of my *sandō* looks like being India – if I ever make it home from here, that is.

7

Thursday

Now I'm breathing more easily and the mask has come off, now I can drink tea, they've moved me. As soon as I began to spiral upwards rather than downwards, they trundled me off down the corridor to this room with three other men.

Next to me is Stan, who reads the newspaper all day every day, barely breaking for the Blessed Sacrament and lunch. Stan has only one leg. Straight across from me is Ziggy, who slumps down in a chair by the window from breakfast until the sun goes, cocooned in the ranting of talkback radio. His visitors look like the sort of people who probably play golf. I can't see who is in the fourth bed, diagonally opposite mine. He never stirs and never speaks. To me his head is just a dark stain on the pale pillow. Fortunately, I am still next to a window facing west towards the city.

Peter has rushed back home again to rescue the dog from the kennels, where her time was up. He's had to drive for hours through snow and sleet this morning across the island from Devonport where the ferry docks. The house was an ice-box when he finally got there, he said, and he couldn't light it or heat it or even telephone at first because high winds had brought down the power lines. Kali is clearly still on the warpath.

Which reminds me: out of nowhere (Canberra) a written message arrived this morning calling down on me the kindness of elephant-headed Ganesh, begging him to keep his 'blissful eye' on me. Mushy invocations to garlanded, pot-bellied deities to look down on me 'kindly like an enchanted young mother' are not the sort of thing that usually cuts much ice with me. In fact, I can feel slightly green around the gills just reading about 'infinite awareness' and 'endless planes of existence'. When I read this message from Canberra, though, my thoughts turned to all the eyes that had been kept on me during the past few days on the tenth floor of St Vincent's, so many eyes, some blissful, some deep-seeing, some amused, both women's and men's eyes,

African eyes, Arab eyes, Chinese eyes, Russian, Polish and Peruvian eyes, Peter's eyes, friends' eyes, at dawn, by day, at dusk, and by night, as I lay here struggling to breathe.

I also thought about elephants. Surrounded by flowers (some of which are pink exactly like Ganesh's) I thought about all those garlanded Ganeshes I'd seen beside doorways in India. And I also thought about the cantering Indian elephant in the miniature on the wall right beside my bed at home. How could I have forgotten him? With his blue-clad mahout brandishing a feathery goad and a rajah in a gold howdah on his back, this bejewelled elephant has been stepping out gaily, draped in an exquisitely embroidered saddle-cloth (crimson, green and gold, finely patterned), perhaps on his way to a durbar festival, his eyes and lips smiling, beside my bed, for decades. He's virtually the first thing I see of a morning, the last I see at night.

'Why,' I asked my well-wisher when I called him (he's the friend of a friend who popped in on me a day or two ago), 'was it Ganesh you turned to when you heard I needed an eye kept on me?'

'Because,' he said, 'Ganesh is a naughty god, and you are very naughty man.'

I broke into one of my rasping cackles, choking for air.

'And he also removes obstacles and blockages,' he said. I instantly pictured his trunk burrowing its way up whichever of my arteries was burrowed up that first night from my groin towards my heart to keep clots at bay. I must say that on the tenth floor of St Vincent's a tender-hearted Ganesh or two amongst the morbid crucifixions on the walls would make a lot of us feel much perkier.

I usually come to towards the end of the afternoon to find Karen and Anthony beside the bed bringing news of the rehearsals. Today, though, when I open my eyes, I can only see Anthony in the gloom. Outside it's turned wet and wintry. The sky looks bruised. Since there are only scraps of me here most afternoons, we'd better talk about my play – about anything, to be honest, to forestall questions about how I'm feeling, but ideally the play.

'Hullo, Anthony,' I say with a woozy smile. 'How long have you been there?' Is he there? I hope so. I hope we both are.

'Not long,' he says. 'Do you like hyacinths?'

I love hyacinths. The splash of Tuareg blue against the clouds on a rainy afternoon like this one is electrifying.

'Tuareg,' I say.

'Pardon?'

Oh, never mind. I hardly know Anthony – well,

I don't really know him at all. I peered up at him a few times as I was sinking, fanunffling at him from under my mask, imagining I was saying things worth saying about what I've written, things that might give him and Karen some idea of what I thought the play was all about when I wrote it, but I don't really know him. Wordlessly I look at him, with a crooked grin he looks at me. 'You look like a craggy Grace Kelly,' he says.

When he puts them into a vase, the hyacinths are luminously, almost preternaturally blue, as if lit from within, against the silvery grey outside. Oh, I think this gentlemanly punk will understand what I mean by infatuation without any prompting at all.

And that's the nub of it, after all: infatuation. That's what this play of mine revolves around. 'Not love,' I mumble, to Anthony's puzzlement, 'that's not the nub of it at all.' (He nods encouragingly.) No, not love, but sudden, unrequited longing. While it's love that tends to hog the limelight these days (and not just Great Loves, either, but any kind of sexual entanglement), it's infatuations, crushes and fleeting obsessions that are usually much more memorable – at least, they are in my experience. Indeed, many of us can recall a brief, lopsided amour when we were sixteen with much greater clarity (and lingering pain) than a marriage lasting decades.

Behind Anthony, who is still waiting patiently for me to form a sentence, if I craned my neck, I could see the bridge to the North Shore, half lost in the bleak drizzle. It was on the other side of that bridge that I once did quite a bit of longing, although more particularly in summer, almost never on a winter's day like this one. In my experience it's in the warmer months that infatuations tend to flourish. Mere lust might raise its head in spring (especially in the seedy night-time streets around this hospital), but the crush or the sudden, rosy attachment, infinitely more nuanced sorts of longing than lust is – often barely carnal – bloom best, mostly agonisingly and lushly, in the sun and heat. And at the height of summer, at least when I was a North Shore teenager, infatuation was rampant at the beach.

Living as I did a long bus and tram ride from the nearest beach, I mostly moped about during the summer holidays like the heroine of a Jane Austen novel, bored, frustrated, waiting for something to happen, something to fill the vacant days, anything at all to disrupt my life's 'well-judged smallness' (to borrow a lethally accurate phrase from *Emma*). Above all I waited to be picked up and taken down to the sea. 'I must beg you,' Emma cries at some family gathering, 'not to talk of the sea. It makes me envious and miserable . . .' I first read *Emma* when I was just eighteen and knew precisely how she felt. The sea, the sea: healthy bodies, vice and appetite. In Austen one goes to balls by the sea to dance and to be eyed. Eventually Emma honeymoons by the sea, doesn't she?

The Austen novels are all a terrible tangle in my head this afternoon, to be honest, but something I do remember very clearly is that it was by the sea, at Sidmouth to be precise (such a strikingly ugly name for a town), where the water could sometimes look pink, and not in the marriage market of Bath where she was living at the time, that Jane Austen fell in love for the only time in her life (that we know of). It was not the closest she came to wedlock, though, which has nothing whatsoever to do with falling in love: it was the following year that she came within a hair's breadth of ending up somebody's wife, the unforgettably named stutterer and all-round dullard Harris Bigg-Wither's wife, to be precise, who was the son of Lovelace Bigg-Wither. I roll these names around on my tongue with voluptuous pleasure: 'Lovelace and Harris Bigg-Wither,' I tell Anthony mysteriously, 'with two g's in Bigg.' After consenting to marry Harris one day, she slept on it and rejected him the next, although he was so rich that most of England would have jumped at the chance, whatever his shortcomings. This was not a seaside dalliance, however: the Bigg-Wither fiasco occurred in the country.

I can remember spending whole muggy weeks yearning to be at the beach – at Manly surfing beach mostly: my equivalent of Emma's Southend or Weymouth – where I knew the object of that month's desire would be sprawled in the sun, oiled and salty, lithe but relaxed, alongside other oiled, salty, lithe but relaxed young things. I would long to be there with them all, ache to touch and be touched, to feel bang in the middle of things, to feel I *was* the middle of things, at least from somebody's point of view; it's not a lot to ask, to feel that bolt of whatever it's called shoot through me – whatever it was that shot through people in books and films – through Marianne Dashwood, for example, in *Sense and Sensibility* when she first clapped eyes on that sultry cad Mr Willoughby. (She called it 'love', and at that age, in my innocence, I was inclined to believe her.)

Not to be there with Them All meant feeling that life itself was happening somewhere else without me – an unbearable feeling when you're a teenager, like drifting all alone through space on a crippled spaceship waiting for the oxygen to run out. Hideous. Sometimes, heading for Manly on the double-decker bus, I'd catch sight of someone – it could be anyone: a man, a child, a boy my age – watering the roses, say, just standing watering the roses in the front yard as I sailed past, and I'd think to myself: *But how can you just stand there, watering the roses like that, unnoticed by . . .* well, by whoever it was whose glance (never mind a kiss) gave me my very being that morning. *Why don't you just kill yourself? Unacknowledged as you are by . . .* by whoever had conjured me out of nothingness and got me on the bus. *What difference would it make?*

When I was a student of nineteen, apropos of nothing I could put my finger on (a grin, perhaps, a laugh, or an easy, sparkling way of being all the things I'd have liked to be but never would) I came down with a particularly bad case of infatuation – unforeseen and totally one-sided, naturally. (If it's reciprocated, it's called something else.) By the summer, with three months of vacation time yawning before me and Christmas gloom already gathering, I was teetering on the verge of insanity. Not only would I be marooned in the stifling hinterland of Sydney for the duration, but the dastardly Mr Willoughby to my chaste Marianne Dashwood (as it were) was setting sail on a tramp to visit some of the more Maugham-ish ports of South-East Asia, places such as Malacca and Kuching and quite possibly somewhere steamy in Sumatra. I no longer remember exactly – places, anyway, that made Lane Cove feel like the most boring backwater on the face of the planet. And to raise the temperature and make things worse, the airwaves were full of Beatles songs that summer. Everyone (except me) seemed to be twisting and shouting and being kept satisfied.

Now, there's only one definitive cure for the listlessness, jealousy and chagrin of the kind afflicting Marianne Dashwood: the prospect of marriage – what we call these days 'a long-term relationship'. In the meantime, however, while waiting for suitable suitors to appear, what Marianne Dashwood did was distract herself with self-improvement. For an Austen heroine this usually means accompanying yourself on the piano, embroidering and visiting the poor between bouts of walking in the rain.

Now and again I would also play the piano – occasionally something German, sometimes a hymn or two, but mostly catchy tunes with playful lyrics from *South Pacific*, *The King and I* and *Oklahoma!*. Cole Porter was another favourite – all those melodious double entendres. (There's always something slightly melancholy, something left-on-the-shelf, about playing the piano alone: married women, as the detestable Mrs Elton observes in *Emma*, never play, being far too occupied with gossiping and good works to practise.)

In place of embroidery, I decided that I, too, needed an accomplishment to tide me over: I would teach myself to type. Week after week I sat and typed. While my Willoughby cavorted with dusky natives in the soft, spice-laden air of . . . well, I didn't want to picture it too specifically, it was too painful, I sat at my desk in Lane Cove and typed. To the sounds of 'Can't Buy Me Love' and 'All My Loving' on my transistor radio, endlessly repeated, I tap-tap-tapped away at my Remington portable. Quick brown foxes by the thousand jumped over lazy black dogs. I typed in the morning, I typed in the afternoon, clickety-clickety-click CLING, clickety-clickety-click CLING, banishing thoughts of Bangkok and Borneo. I typed poems and short stories, I typed essays. I typed a short dissertation on Tolstoy.

One day I had a breakthrough: I no longer knew where the letters were on the keyboard – only my fingers knew. I could touch-type! It was like being reborn. It was a transfiguration. I was now *homo typens*. By the end of February I could type almost as fast as I could talk. It changed my life: ever since, for half a century, first at typewriters and then at computer screens, I have sat and watched my thoughts turn effortlessly, unthinkingly, into script. English thoughts, French thoughts, Russian thoughts: I sit, I tap and there they are before me, my thoughts incarnate. It's a kind of alchemy.

Few summers have stayed with me with such heart-aching clarity as that one has. There have been other crushes since, naturally. At different points, mostly between late October and mid-March, I have been infatuated, moonstruck, even close to cuckoo with desire (just briefly). I have even been married, which is quite different. But the clack of a typewriter, a bar or two of 'She Loves You' and the summer of 1964 comes flooding back in vivid detail, the summer when longing first reached fever pitch, threatening to derange me, but in the nick of time was turned into typing.

As time goes by, I find that infatuation can strike in almost any setting, although rarely on trams. That said, I'm always mindful of the fact that E. M. Forster was famously and powerfully smitten on a tram in Alexandria, colouring the attitude to trams of a multitude of men ever since. (Anthony is looking baffled. Have I just said 'tram'?) Rarely at the beach, either, since my youth. If I bring to mind the detailed list I keep in a drawer at home of my major adult infatuations, it strikes me that, while there is quite a variety of locations mentioned in the WHERE column, there is only one mention of a beach. There's an airliner over Germany (twice), there's a dinner party in Paris (11th arrondissement, high above the railway yards), there's a Turkish bath, there's . . . but wait a minute: running my mind's eye down the list, I can see that ever since my thirties the place in which I've been most likely to come undone is foyers. Yes, it's definitely in foyers that I've been most at risk of falling prey to a savage liking for someone lithe and mischievous (particularly theatre foyers or art gallery foyers), at a pinch in libraries (but that was also in Paris). I'm not talking about an urgent desire for sexual intimacy, I'm talking about an impulsive and sometimes brutal *sympathie* (always misjudged) for someone I've just met. I have in mind the abrupt willingness to like someone I don't know at all with a fraction too much intimacy too soon. Come to think of it, it was in foyers (of a certain kind, not bank foyers – each to his own) that I first came under the spell of more than one of the visitors to this very bedside. What is it about these foyers and becoming besotted, I wonder? Even in Jane Austen's novels, theatres and their 'lobbies' seethe with erotic possibility – Astley's in Lambeth, the Haymarket and the Theatre Royal, Drury Lane. Foyers were as much about eyeing (and eyeing off) as ballrooms. Anthony leans over towards me, with a quizzical look on his face. I may have just muttered 'foyer' or even 'Lambeth'?

In theatre and art gallery foyers you suspect you're amongst kindred spirits, that's the thing. Here, you imagine, a spot of sympathetic *darshan*, as Prakash might put it, will not be out of the question – although nothing too focused, nothing too clear-eyed, as might happen around a dinner table or in a café. For infatuation to blossom, room must always be left for misapprehension and the play of semblances; the possibility of having made a ghastly mistake must always be thrillingly present. There's a flightiness, a fleetingness, a fugitive quality to the interlocking glances in the kind of vestibule I have in mind that's perfect for hatching an infatuation. They're like the butterflies, these glances, in the butterfly house I once visited in Kuala Lumpur. You never know where a butterfly will alight next – on that orchid, on your own nose.

More than that: in a certain kind of foyer a hunger for something new ripples through the crowd (and through you) – new and *in some sense of the word* beautiful. Yes, here you can believe you are surrounded by people who appreciate beauty – in art or in landscapes or in movement or animals or language or feelings. To be struck by another's beauty (*in some sense of the word*, as I say) and to want to weave a story around it, however briefly, which is the essence of infatuation, you must first appreciate beauty in this wider sense. In art gallery or theatre foyers in particular – even in an art gallery shop or at the coffee counter or in a queue for tickets (a ticket-queue, in my experience, is almost calamitously risky if you're this way inclined) – you can often feel imaginations waking up and colouring, ready to dovetail with other imaginations. You rarely get that in malls, buses or even hotel foyers – or at least not reliably. In my Syrian diary, I remember now, I noted how unattracted I was to the handsome and flirtatious young men inhabiting the foyer of my scruffy hotel in Palmyra – *because I did not believe in their powers of imagination.* That's what I wrote at the time, just before the bloodshed began. Perhaps I was mistaken, or perhaps our imaginations were just so different they could never mesh, but that's how I explained to myself the lack of any first flutter of appetite, any first tightening of the throat. For that to happen, you need to believe in imaginations brushing up against each other and starting to catch. And so, on returning towards evening from a day spent alone amongst the ruins, I was happy to banter with them in the still, hot air, but I was quite unmoved. They were almost violently charming.

There was probably another factor at play here as well – what I nowadays think of as the Donald Richie factor (coming back to Richie): single travellers, Richie writes (in his book about travelling alone around the Inland Sea), often feel that they should pick somebody up for sex because, against all expectation, there is never quite enough to do when you travel, whatever the brochures might claim, especially once it gets dark. Leisure in the highest sense is such a refined art. Richie wants not so much to have sex or to embark on the long and tiresome ritual that might, but probably will not, lead to 'this faintly desired end', but to have already had sex. How refreshing to have someone admit it! And he was twenty-five years younger than I was in Palmyra when he wrote this. Richie, of course, lived in Japan where, thanks to the warp of Shinto, and despite the weft of Buddhism, there is not the same anxiety about sex you find embedded in most other cultures.

Am I hopelessly old-fashioned in all this? At my age and in my condition an actual exchange of glances with anyone at all is a lot to hope for, that goes without saying, but I'm tempted to think that the very notion of infatuation may be on the wane these days. In an era of apps for instantly locating sexual partners, finding yourself spellbound in this way may be as *passé* as the horse and cart. Not only in modern English, but in contemporary French as well, the very words people once used for these subtle feelings are beginning to sound archaic – 'crush', 'besotted', *'béguin'*, *'épris'* and so on. Who talks like this in the twenty-first century? A barely acknowledged undertow of longing may not be fashionable any more, may be no longer 'cool'.

I consider Anthony against the thickening lilac of the clouds. He's a lot younger than I am, but no boy. As a theatre director, I'm sure his heart has been unexpectedly broken in many a foyer over the years. He grins again. We neither of us speak. I think he's still waiting for me to finish some sentence or other. I have the vague feeling that I might have said out loud *'béguin, épris'*.

My mind drifts back to the foyer at the Stables Theatre just up the road from where we are: in that cramped foyer with its red-painted concrete floor, half a lifetime ago, while serving the coffee at interval, I once became instantly obsessed with litheness and stayed in the grip of my baneful, mad obsession for well over a year. That's because at that time – and this is important – I was not already loved. Obsessions, I can't help thinking, especially when they turn into addictions, are usually woven around a vacuum.

Run-of-the-mill infatuations, on the other hand, are able to take flight, I do believe, sails billowing, most spectacularly when the affections are already securely anchored, the heart spoken for – when you already love and are loved. This is little understood. Sometimes people say to me: ah, well, I don't fall victim to infatuations because I have Malcolm (or Janet or Kevin or Jane). But don't you see? I want to say back (but don't). It's *because* Malcolm (or Janet or Kevin or Jane) has your heart that you can allow yourself this kind of joy (and the pain that goes with it). Ivan Sergeyevich Turgenev (such a mouthful of a name) understood all this perfectly. The love of his life, Pauline Viardot, Madame Viardot, mother of four, mezzo soprano, toast of Europe, did not, but he did. It was while reading about Turgenev's infatuation with a young actress when he was sixty (perhaps older, I can't remember) that I came up with the idea for my play. It revolves around Turgenev – and a theatre and a train. The nineteenth-century railway compartment, with its illusion of intimacy, the chance to make conversation, the exchange of glances, must have hatched infatuations by the thousand all over the world.

So it's thanks to Turgenev that I am lying here alive and Anthony is sitting beside me, the blue of his hyacinths slicing through the thickening murk into my quick. 'Hyacinths,' I say aloud, 'so beautiful.'

In my mind, though, what I say is: it's all true, you know. It's *because* he loved Pauline Viardot with all his heart, and had done, unwaveringly, since he first heard her sing in the Alexandrinsky Theatre in St Petersburg at the age of twenty-five, and would do until the moment he died (no infatuation this); it was *because* she also, in her own way, despite being married for all that time and loving her husband deeply and without reserve, gave her heart to him (this being no mere passing attachment on her part, either); it was *because they loved each other*, in other words, that Turgenev could allow himself to be so smitten by the young actress Marya Gavrilovna Savina (who was no beauty, by the way – slightly common, if anything, a touch swarthy, with a servant's voice), could permit himself to be so idiotically 'carried away', as they say in Russian. Carried away in a train with her as well for just one hour, as it happens, on the twenty-eighth of May 1880. He joined her on the train at Mtsensk at her invitation and left her an hour later at Oryol.

Infatuations are always about beginnings. Nobody knows what happened in her compartment during that hour, but the beginning led nowhere. Infatuations don't lead anywhere – that's the beauty of them. If they lead somewhere, they're called something else. Biographers have cogitated on what might have happened. Julian Barnes wrote a long essay about it. But nobody knows. My play is built around this hour in the train. I could have called it *The Hour*, instead of *A Mad Affair*. But since in my version this encounter is retold by a modern-day madman, perhaps *A Mad Affair* is as good a title as any.

'Infatuation is not love, you see,' I say to Anthony in that slightly pompous way I have. 'But you know that.' That's when I realise he has actually been speaking for some time. I can't get a proper grasp on what he's saying, though. I clutch at it, but it keeps sliding past me into silence. I peer at him, but I can't see him very well against the blur of mauvish light. It's then that I see that he's turned himself into a woman in a white coat.

'I'm sorry,' I say, 'I mistook you for Anthony.'

'Cup of tea?'

'Don't mind if I do. With a biscuit, if you have any.' I live for these cups of tea with two biscuits, now they're permitted.

Evening gathers.

Ziggy's daughter, a young woman in trousers with a backpack, definitely on the move, has just arrived to sit with him. He rouses himself, switches off his radio. The little waves of loathing and anger that usually surge from it to lap around him ebb. He's not quite as old as I am, but grey-haired and far from svelte. Still with us, but not vividly present. They watch television together in sporadic silence for half an hour as the day outside fades, and then she leaves. As she passes she gives me an unreadable smile.

In the bed next to me, Stan, who shot his leg off while duck-shooting, it's transpired, appears to be in particularly good spirits this evening. I have never been this close to a duck-shooter before, being more a gatherer than a hunter myself. I try to imagine what it must be like to be someone who enjoys firing bullets into ducks, but can't. (These days I do little seeking of any kind, strictly speaking, let alone hunting: I mostly wait to be ambushed.) A mottled man about my own age, Stan isn't doing too well, but usually he's quite matey – after all, we're men with a common enemy: a treacherous heart – but completely incurious. Likes a laugh.

As night falls, everyone tends to watch Channel 7 in silence. Tonight a young man in the fourth bed over near the door is staring up at the television screen where it hangs from the ceiling, with half a dozen members of his family arrayed around him smelling strongly of takeaway food. The television set is like a household shrine. It demands daily silent devotion. Here they are, these three men, possibly coming to the last of their succession of days, and of their own free will they're spending them watching Channel 7.

'Fucking refugees,' I hear Stan mutter, eyes glued to the screen. 'They've got the whole country by the balls.' The ward goes silent. Then someone starts barking at Ziggy and Stan. He's yapping and ranting like the voices on Ziggy's radio. I can feel a ragged thumping in my

84

chest. I'm going to have another heart attack. Perhaps I've already had it because I seem to be floating above my bed observing this small, gaunt figure under the covers below me flapping his hands and hurling abuse at Ziggy and Stan, and that, according to a woman I saw recently on television, is precisely what happens when you die for good: you float upwards and see things on top of the wardrobe you'd never known were there. 'You're morons, both of you,' he's yelling, 'gobbling down that crazy shit they feed you every day, you're brain-dead lumps of stinking . . .' Oh, no, I'm definitely going into cardiac arrest again here. I can't think of an appropriate noun to go with 'stinking'. I can't breathe. '. . . scum!' I shout. (Can you have 'lumps of stinking scum'?)

'You sound just like my daughter,' Ziggy says morosely.

'I'm terribly sorry,' I mumble, floating down into my body again and taking deep breaths. 'I don't know what came over me.'

'That's quite alright.'

'I do apologise.'

'End of story, mate,' Stan says, 'end of story.'

The group around the fourth bed pretends nothing has happened.

The Peruvian nurse with one continuous eyebrow brings us our trays. I do love hospital food – airline food as well, I must admit, school lunches, college trifles, anything institutional. I love the way the meal has been miniaturised, I adore the crudely coloured jellies and insipid broths, I salivate over the lukewarm spaghetti bolognese, excited by the way the fuggy smell of it wafts up the corridor ahead of it. With greedy pleasure I wolf down my fish with tomato and basil, and then start in on my tub of mass-produced custard. Whole vats of the stuff bubbling away downstairs, probably, in the kitchens in the basement. It's delicious. I am reborn, I am a child again. To the west, beyond the old prison beyond the trees beyond the windows of my corner of the ward, the sky has miraculously cleared. The gleaming slabs of glass I keep my eye on all day soar up into the peerless apricot sky of early evening.

I miss Peter. I miss the dog. Out of the billions, trillions of people and animals in the world, I miss, at this precise moment, just these two.

8

Friday

What day is it? I'm losing track. Scott came in again to see me this morning, but I didn't like to ask him. So here I lie, in a jumble of sheets across from one-legged Stan and the snoring Ziggy, making my way in little bursts through David Lodge's novel *Deaf Sentence*. Peter picked it up for me in Oxford Street just before he went home. He said that it's just what you want a dose of in a hospital ward: English wit. Until this morning, though, I haven't been up to it.

Quite unexpectedly, to my intense joy, another snook is cocked at randomness: *days*. There's that word again!

What are days for?
Days are where we live.
They come, they wake us
Time and time over.
They are to be happy in:
Where can we live but days?

Ah, solving that question
Brings the priest and the
  doctor
In their long coats
Running over the fields.

                    Philip Larkin

How astounding! Lodge's narrator quotes a poem by Philip Larkin called, of all things, 'Days'. I buck up on the spot. *What are days for?* Well, exactly! What indeed? I'm itching to share the moment with somebody, but Ziggy and I don't speak (although if I leant forward far enough I could practically swat him with my *National Geographic*), while Stan, who occasionally asks me what I think of the fucking greenies, is unlikely to be interested. In the far bed today there's a mute Korean.

I don't find the poem disheartening at all, by the way. The novel's narrator does, and David Lodge might, too, but I don't, not for a minute. On the contrary, it *gives* me heart. I don't know a lot about Philip Larkin, not being much of a one for poetry, having found so little of it transporting, but I do know that he rarely gives anyone heart. He skewers, pricks, amuses, lances, stuns. He was too aware that, while most things might never happen, death certainly would, to give anyone heart. All we can do, from Larkin's perspective, I gather, is ruefully endure.

But this morning I can do more than that: I can simply enjoy myself. I have endured. *For the time being* I need not contemplate anything except the euphoric upswing of convalescence. Even if Larkin's doctors are running across the fields towards me in their long coats to tell me that, in the final analysis, I'm not getting better at all, nobody my age is – that's what old age is, after all: the process of irrevocably getting worse, not better – even so, today I *feel* as if I'm soaring, I feel as if I've just scored a GET OUT OF JAIL FREE card, I feel almost weightless, I feel undeniably much, much better. Yes, little by little 'the million-petalled flower / Of being here' – another phrase of Larkin's – may indeed be losing its vibrant hues and shrivelling up, but it can be contemplated with pleasure for what it is today.

Larkin wrote 'Days', it seems, while still a youngish man (several decades short of dying, at any rate), a librarian at the University of Hull. To my mind, Hull has a hopeless, downwards feel to it, like Scunthorpe, just across the Humber, although I've never been to either of them. Not quite as wretched as Hemel Hempstead, say, or Slough, Hull nonetheless makes you think of rust and old factories covered in graffiti. 'Man jailed for chainsaw attack in Hull pub' is what came up when Scott googled Hull on his telephone. But I don't find this poem Hullish. Godless, obviously – the scurrying priests at the end looking like clowns – even a touch macabre, but not despairing or dour.

What are days for? You can almost hear a little boy turning to his father and asking, 'Daddy, what are days for?' Curiously enough, it strikes me this morning as a more sophisticated question than the clichéd, more adult 'What is the meaning of life?'

After avoiding the question for three lines – 'Well, days are just there', 'Days just happen, one after the other' – Larkin suggests with a certain faux non-chalance that what days are for is 'to be happy in' (as if we all knew what 'happy' meant). Really? It's a comfortingly optimistic thing to say – after all, without something akin to optimism, why would you let yourself be woken time and time over? I mean, why would you bother living another day? Ziggy over there, slumped greyly in his chair, doesn't look optimistic about either himself or the world outside, but he's clearly choosing to live another day, so he must think it's worthwhile hoping for *something* – for the government to be thrown out, for interest rates to skyrocket, *something*. God knows why Stan agrees to be woken 'time and time over', but he probably feels embedded in a family happiness narrative of some Northern Beaches kind – yes, he's very likely borne along on that, day after day after day. One-legged he may be, not to mention addicted to the *Daily Telegraph* and the

Eucharist, but I feel a pang of envy. What am *I* optimistic about at this delicate point in my slow *dégringolade* (more elegant in French, but still a downhill tumble) towards the abyss?

Narrative itself is such an optimistic form, when you come to think about it. Is that why I'm reading a novel in the first place? It's not a Pollyanna-ish form, it's not devoid of unravellings and pain, but it's optimistic in the sense that you keep turning the pages (or writing them), one after the other, 'time and time over', in the hope of something transforming happening. Isn't that it? In the hope of a transforming answer *to your particular questions*. (What are mine? They're not Stan's or Ziggy's, I'm sure, let alone Phillip Adams's or the Archbishop of Canterbury's, or even Peter's, but there's a swarm of them buzzing around my head all day every day, I'm forever batting one or other of them out of the way so I can concentrate on something more trivial.) That's all I would say: something transforming. Not even necessarily transformingly beautiful. Just transfigurative. I've puzzled for years about why some fine writers leave me caring little about whether or not I turn the page – indeed, why sometimes, even though I feel as a writer that I've said something well, I also feel it wasn't worth saying, that I may as well have gone out and dead-headed the roses. I think it's usually because there is no hope of transformation in what I'm reading or writing – or, more exactly, no hope of transforming answers to the particular questions I ask.

Within the framework of the day, I can hope, that's the point. Plainly my life *as a whole* is hopeless, something I barely foresaw when I was younger. Well, I mean, *look at me, for God's sake!* I startle Stan, erupting in a sloshing laugh. A well-shaped day, on the other hand, is not hopeless at all. But what is a well-shaped day? Larkin doesn't say.

He moves in for the kill now with another, less childlike, question, which he mischievously omits to answer: 'Where can we live but days?' What choice, in other words, do we have but to live from day to day? Indeed, what else can we do but inhabit passing time – keep turning the pages, as it were? Commit suicide, I expect, but apart from that, what?

It's so bracing when somebody asks you outright what few have the courage to ask. In this regard Zadie Smith's Mrs Kipps leaps to mind. In *On Beauty*, which I've just been reading, Mrs Kipps asks very bald questions indeed. For example: 'Now what do you think of my house?' The well-heeled woman that Mrs Kipps is speaking to is brought up short: although it's implicit in every exchange she has with other women about their houses, it is a question that is simply never fired at you point-blank like that. Mrs Kipps, though, is almost dead, so inclined to speak bluntly.

I squirm with pleasure and look about me. Finally free of my oxygen mask and trailing no more than half a dozen cannulae, I now can. I study the complexion of the day. A lemony sunlight is washing over my corner of the ward. Larkin has just looked me straight in the eye and said: forget years, forget lifetimes and the shapes they've taken on, it's a succession of *days* you live in, so make sure they're good ones, be happy in them *as they pass,* one after the other, that's the point. That's where we live – not so much in Hobart or Hull in this year or that, not even in lifetimes, let alone 'in the moment' (how fatuous) or in God's timeless gaze, as in our own succession of days. *Learn to value that.* Or as David Lodge puts it (a touch drily, possibly) at the very end of this novel of his: 'try to value the passing time'. I *am* trying, Professor Lodge, believe me, but, God in heaven, it's hard.

What you've written is all very well, Professor, but in what way should I spend my days in order to make them worth valuing as they glide by? In whatever way makes me 'happy'? I stare at the line of glassy skyscrapers to the west. Reading thought-provoking books in the sun? Meeting friends who set me alight with flares of conversation? Darting off when I can to spend a week somewhere I can time-travel – to a garden by the lake in Udaipur, for instance, or to Fez, say, deep in the medina amongst all the minarets and calls to prayer (and other kinds of calls, as I remember, the further down the hill you go into the thick of it)? Slaking my frenzied desires? (Are any of my desires still frenzied?)

None of that is enough, though, is it. There's something to it, but it's not nearly enough. Happiness is not enough. Only wanting what you can have – which is what happiness is – is not enough. There's not enough there to value as the days fly past. *Besides, the geometrics are all wrong*, and when you're older, apart from anything else, you need a new geometry for your days – nothing too overwrought and convoluted, but nothing too overarching, either. So how can I spend my days in order to make them worth valuing as they pass?

Like most people I know, I've spent most of my days trying either to ignore time's passing or to weave intricately patterned tapestries out of the years and decades (as you probably have to do when you're younger). Now and again I've also tried to tap time on the head with a magic wand, setting off small explosions of timeless bliss in tiny salvos: *pop! pop! pop!* This is not, by the way, at all the same thing as maundering around in a bog of fatuous *carpe diem*s or living as if today were the last day in your life. I saw *Dead Poets Society* in 1989 – everyone saw it (well, apart from Stan, perhaps) – and so naturally, along with everyone else, I briefly considered seizing the day, as Robin Williams told his pupils to do. However, not being an American teenager at the time, I realised almost straight away that days can't be seized. As Seneca said somewhere or other with his usual directness: why waste your time? Even though you seize it, it will still flee. Precisely – that's the whole point about time: it's a dimension, not a thing, so you can't *seize* bits of it, except in retrospect, where it lies about in pinches, lumps and little piles of shards. It's what you *do* with your days that matters.

What does Ziggy think is a good way to spend his days in order to value them as they pass? Does he ever consider it? If the Eucharist is anything to go by, Stan is hoping that we don't *only* live in a succession of days, but still, what does he think his days are for while he's still here? I feel confident that watching a Hungarian classic on SBS is a better way to pass time than watching the umpteenth repeat of an American sitcom on Channel 7. But why is it better? Why is reading *Deaf Sentence* by David Lodge a better way to inhabit the days than nodding off over the *Daily Telegraph* and then gulping down a wafer and mouthful of wine? (David Lodge, come to think of it, is not averse to receiving the Blessed Sacrament from time to time, either, or at least was once not averse to it, and in Stan's position might well go through the motions himself, just on the off-chance.) Yet I'm sure it is. My whole life has been predicated on the assumption that it's better, as have all my friends' lives. For the moment, as I lie here, I can't remember *why* I've been so sure about this all my life, but I have.

However, I have largely failed to live in my succession of days, I can see that now. My time's nearly up, and I have squandered decades. '*I wasted time, and now doth time waste me . . .*' (*Richard II*, North Sydney Boys High School, just across the bridge over there, 1960. I understood *nothing*.) On the rare occasions when I have in some measure succeeded, it's been because underneath the shopping, washing and cleaning that daily life consists of; underneath all the forgettable detective novels I've read (along with the odd classic, usually Continental) and interchangeable episodes of *Midsomer Murders*; underneath the mountain of book reviews I've read and written, the unremarkable dinners with friends, the twice-daily outings with the dog, the tens of thousands of weather and news reports I've watched, the lifetime of sitting about in bus shelters and airport lounges, the hours, days, weeks and months spent just waiting for the lights to change at the end of our street; if I have succeeded, as I say, in living in my succession of days, it's because underneath all that dailiness, I've glimpsed cluster after meshing cluster of experience – whole chasms of them, down, down, down they go into the depths of memory, criss-crossing and feeding into each other until they fade from view in the murk of my unconscious – and now and again tumbled down into them, somersaulting wide-eyed into their depths.

Layers, that's the key, as I putter – indeed, sputter – towards death, I think to myself. Layers are the new geometry: thickly layered days in which I am my own master.

I freeze (as it were) in a shaft of sunlight: it's the days full of layered time that are worth the most, the days when I've lived many lives between breakfast and falling asleep. Why has this never struck me before? The thing about Channel 7 is that it rarely adds to the layers of selves to plumb. It's patently not *enough*, this layering, not *enough* to make a life worth having been lived, but without it the day is not worth living in. Here I am looking out at the city, for example, yet beneath the prosaic city beyond my window there's a layering of other cities, invisible exactly like those ancient oasis towns lost for centuries beneath the featureless sands of the Gobi and Taklamakan deserts. Out there beneath the everyday are the buried grids of earlier cities I was born and lived out my life in, cities of the mind, or perhaps, more accurately, now I come to think about it, cities I've given my heart to over the years, crammed with glowing treasures, like those cities in Chinese Turke-stan. These are layered webs of affection, though, each with its own geometry – they are not just middens of haphazard memories.

Yes, it's hard for me not to feel a fondness for those streets far below, for Darlinghurst, despite its whorishness: I could peel back the palimpsests of that city out there one after the other forever, it seems to me now – only in my mind, of course, it's nothing more than the well of memory. There is always the hint of just one more image beneath the one I'm contemplating.

But perhaps I'm only remembering versions of the standard myths we humans spin about ourselves: a virtually Immaculate Conception over at Crown Street Women's Hospital; then the Stolen Prince, when I was whisked away across the bridge; the Burning Bush when I was ten; Love at First Sight . . . Even so, a minute at my window here on the tenth floor could last for decades. One day 'with the Lord' is 'as a thousand years', after all. (And by the same token 'a thousand years are as one day'.) And that's what you want in a cardiothoracic ward at nearly seventy.

Once in a waiting room at Tunis Airport, on that first trip with Scott to North Africa, the man across from me began to play 'Silent Night' on the flute he had with him, although it wasn't even Christmas, while the American woman sitting next to me explained to her companion how the subjunctive worked in French. It was like sliding the cover off a deep pool and leaping into it, I was ecstatic . . . sinking down through all those steamy Christmases when I was small in Lane Cove, each more disappointing than the one before, each a sad lesson in the hopelessness of any stab I might make at celebration (although I was happy enough reading the paperback edition of *Seven Years in Tibet* that my parents gave me for Christmas one year, falling in love for the first time with the Himalayas, with lost lands, with utter foreignness) . . . and then I heard us singing the carol in German at school (*Stille Nacht, heilige Nacht, / Alles schläft; einsam wacht / Nur das traute hochheilige Paar* . . . something something something) . . . and that brought 'Lili Marleen' to mind . . . *Wie einst, Lili Marleen, wie einst Lili Marleen* . . . Marlene Dietrich was singing it smokily, and singing 'Falling in Love Again' as well, something I did more than once (I often fell in love, I mean) within sight of this tenth-floor window . . . *Ich bin von Kopf bis Fuss auf Liebe eingestellt* . . . *Falling in love again, never wanted to. What am I to do – can't help it.* Indeed. And snap-snap-snap inside my head, all my can't-help-its kaleidoscoped chaotically, going back decades, going back to when I was just sixteen, each frame so vivid, unspooling, unspooling . . . and in the background I could hear my father speaking French – he didn't speak it with much flair, but he was a stickler for the subjunctive . . . These were not just recollections, these were things I gave my heart to . . . and then I zigzagged back up inside the moment, homing in on the electric blue scarf of the Tuareg in the corner, a conflagration of all the blues I'd ever known . . . Yes, that instant at Tunis Airport was exquisitely layered time.

'How are we feeling?' a woman in white says to me.

I say something wet and muffled.

'He'll be here on Sunday,' she says mysteriously. She seems to be putting something into or taking something out of my arm.

'Who will?'

'Peter – your friend Peter.'

'Ah! Speaking of love at first sight.' Which I was, wasn't I? 'Although if truth be told . . .'

'Pardon?'

'Never mind.' I must try to speak more clearly. 'Peter. That's good news.'

Isn't it? She just smiles and feels for a pulse.

Isn't it?

'Is that the meal trolley I can hear?'

It turns out to be a man with a wheelchair, come to whisk me and my drips away somewhere. 'This won't take long,' he says. 'You'll be back in half an hour.'

'Where are we going?'

'First floor.' That is never good news. Is he Scottish? Sturdy forearms. Off we set. The day suddenly flies apart. I am gone for rather longer than half an hour.

9

Saturday night

'*Nurse! Nurse! Nurse! Nurse!*' Night has fallen. But which one? Saturday? Peter hasn't come back, so it must still be Saturday. It's dead quiet in here, apart from the woman in the next ward calling endlessly for the nurse, as she always does. Out there in Darlinghurst in the darkness by this time on a night like this, even in midwinter, things will be hopping, but in here there's a hush. '*Nurse! Nurse! Nurse! Nurse!*' she caws hoarsely, reminding me of the wattlebird in my back garden. There's a tiny break, like a hiccup, then she starts up again: '*Nurse! Nurse! Nurse! Nurse! Nurse!*'

Ten floors down, the night's detritus is presumably beginning to wash up amongst the soft-drink machines and rows of plastic seats, as it does at about this time every Saturday night (I'm told): it's where I washed up myself last weekend. Down there in Emergency at this very minute they'll be lurching through the doors, outraged and frightened, to vomit and bleed and piss and fight and scream abuse; they'll be staggering and hobbling around the crowded room, trying to remember who they are, moaning and crying out in pain. Some will be dying quietly to the sinister beep of monitors, others noisily, surrounded by bellowing, abusive friends, a few where they've flopped on the floor. It's Saturday night at St Vincent's Hospital. That's just what happens, apparently, at public hospitals in the inner city on the weekends. Not that St Vincent himself would have been fazed, I'm sure, by the savagery and mayhem: he'd have seen much worse when he was a slave in Tunis or chaplain to the galley slaves in France. Having led a softer, even cosseted life, I can't believe it's happening right now in rooms below where I am lying, and will happen there again next weekend, and the weekend after that for centuries to come, perhaps forever, and not just there but all over the world – well, not in Tunis, for self-evident reasons, not these days, not quite like this, but all over Christendom, certainly. Without a doubt in Hemel Hempstead and Hull, for instance. From up here on the tenth floor, however, Saturday night is a frozen cascade of lights to the west, etched with an icy brilliance into the black of the sky, soundless, beautiful past all imagining.

Hemel Hempstead. Hull. Larkin. *Where can we live but days?*

Yes, well, that's the nub of it, isn't it. Where indeed? Ask that question and they all come running.

In years and decades would be one option, but that makes time race by. And in other people's memories (a popular bit of pap). But that's hardly a satisfactory answer to Larkin's question – achieving immortality in other people's memories is pious humbug. It's also been voguish for a long time now to talk about 'living in the moment'. I can see why goldfish might take to this idea, but it strikes me as a witless approach to passing time for humans: the asylum my mother was locked away in at the end of her life was chock-a-block full of people who were living in the moment – in nanoseconds, some of them, although in those days we didn't have nanoseconds. Her neighbour Ronnie from up the corridor, for instance, banged out 'I'm just a girl who cain't say no' on the piano all day every day for eight hours at a stretch because he was living in the moment. Mrs Chew, who hadn't had a visitor in over ten years, was still waiting for her mother to pick her up from school that afternoon in mid-October 1938 when the

Japanese entered Canton. (She never did.) Yes, you *can* live in the moment, but why would you want to?

Where can we live but days? I gaze out at the cold, black sky to consider the options. We can live in eternity, I suppose, if we're to believe the shouts of Larkin's 'priests' as they come running towards us across the fields. Everyone, it seems, has heard the rumours. Never mind the ancient Egyptians or the Chinese: tens of thousands of years ago, before there was an Egypt or a China, the Aborigines believed in an afterlife in a sky-world peopled by ghosts. I gather there's a growing conviction amongst paleoanthropologists that even some Neanderthals in Europe imagined an afterlife for the dead.

STAN: Whatcha say, mate?

ME: Paleoanthropologists.

STAN: Yeah, right. (*Under breath*) Farking hell.

(*Noises off: 'Nurse! Nurse! Nurse! Nurse!'*)

Some Australian Aboriginal peoples, for instance, fancied that the spirits of the dead flourished in a sky-world to the west and, like the moon, occasionally reappeared from there. Others used to picture a self that wandered the world and the sky at night in dreams, meeting the dead (as we all do in our dreams) and coming back to the body on earth in the morning. Through sorcery this self at some point found itself unable to return to the body. This was death. It was unjust. It was unnatural. The spirit in question could become very angry. What was natural, apparently, was some kind of nightly to-ing and fro-ing between different worlds, a to-ing and fro-ing that always eventually comes to a distressing end. These days none of the world's major religions seem to favour coming and going. They all appear to plump for some version or other of 'now you're here, then you're somewhere else'. At the folk level there might be a bit of shilly-shallying between the *here* and the *there* (a penchant for ghosts is surprisingly widespread, as it is for saints and godlets with a foot in both camps), but not at a more refined, intellectual level – at least, not here. I'm not very good with stories about Dreamtime heroes, souls paddling canoes or walking along sunbeams – anything like that. I hanker after something a bit more transcendent. At least when educated Hindus tell this kind of story, you get the impression that they're just doing it to make the ineffable more vivid. Obviously the ineffable can't be rationally explained or it wouldn't be ineffable, but you can at least try to bring it to life.

To be frank, all anyone wants to know these days is what I saw while not living. Even some of Larkin's doctors come running to ask – coyly, as a rule, pretending it's just a joke, but they do ask. 'Did you see any bright lights?' I was asked by a gastroenterologist just the other day. 'Do you mean Jesus?' I asked.

'Jesus, lights – anything at all, really . . . or just nothing?'

A Jewish friend with little time for either Jesus or bright lights, after the routine bit of banter about whether or not anybody had been waiting for me on the other side, asked if I'd at least seen 'a blank' (*probyel* was the Russian word she used – a gap, a blank). Can you *see* a blank? 'Was there anything there?' is what they all want to know, with just the faintest of embarrassed smirks. Where? What makes them think there's a 'there'? It's the wrong question.

Why this obsession with an afterlife? I blame the moon for it all, for this brouhaha about what happens to the bit of you that isn't plant-like or rock-like. Not long before sunset on my first day of new life, the day before Peter arrived, in the amber wash of the sky above the towers to the west, I watched the young crescent moon float down to disappear behind the light-spangled slabs of glass. That first evening it was all I had to watch. The waxing moon and the spangling of the glass. I'd rarely thought about the moon. And at that point I hadn't understood the practically aphrodisiac effect of taking pleasure in the complexion of the sky, the day's face (even at night). At that point, on the first day of my new life, I had still not understood the importance of the day.

When you first see the young moon after nights of

moonlessness – just an almond-coloured sliver of a thing way to the west, a moment or two after sunset – you think to yourself: the moon's not dead after all, it's just been playing hide and seek with us; I've just caught sight of it – no more than a flicker – above the horizon in the west. (Well, not really, that's not what you think to yourself at all these days, but you can imagine someone thinking that, you can imagine someone smiling after a few nights of darkness like the darkness at the bottom of the sea, thinking to himself, 'The moon's not dead after all!') It's what I thought when I was just back myself from . . . Well, not so much back *from* anywhere, perhaps, more *here again*, like the moon, alight again, reflecting back again the light that was striking it. And now, after only a week or so, it's hanging big and buttery above us as the sun goes down. In a week's time, when I wake after midnight, there it will be, at its zenith, still trailing the sun.

Apropos of eternity and transcendence, it was just across the road from where I'm lying and around the corner that I once ardently pursued eternity myself – or timelessness, to be more precise: timelessness and spacelessness, the art of seeing through the glass of time and space still darkly but with hope and wonder. (Para-doxically, I felt more intensely present, firmly anchored in the world, than I do now.) Not *only* around the corner on Sunday mornings, organ music washing over me in vivifying waves, but *also* there, especially there. My affinity for Mary Baker Eddy's view of the world was an entertaining eccentricity my parents quite happily allowed me. More than one strangeness would have caused concern, but one was permitted. They did not live to see my other strangenesses take shape.

How outmoded it all seems now, this interest in radical spirituality. Nobody could care less about this sort of thing nowadays when bushwalking or a bit of homeopathy is about as 'spiritual' as most people seem to get. The word 'spiritual' seems to me to have broken free of any sort of semantic tethering at all. On television one regularly hears psychotic mass murderers referred to as 'spiritual leaders'. One well-known radio personality claimed a while ago to feel 'spiritual' when he looked at the stars. I imagine he meant awe-struck and small.

Yet I feel slightly wistful for those years, as I understand many Westerners of my generation do. I do not regret a second of them. It may all have been 'solemn nonsense' (in Alan Bennett's phrase – not that he's an expert witness); it may all have amounted to a muffled boom signifying nothing, as Mrs Moore in *A Passage to India* believes all the 'divine words' of 'poor little talkative Christianity' do, like conversations in a cave (and, God knows, my version of Christianity was very talkative); it could well have been a daft attempt to tie that mischievous floating signifier 'spiritual' down to something specific and real; but for me it was also a source of intense beauty. Its minimalist, almost Quakerish, beauty was of the essence – it bore me up.

Colourless though this may sound to many, or at best pale blue, especially to those who love nothing more than a gaudy flash or two of red and gold, with a few mitres and crosiers shining in the vaulted half-light, my religion was a sort of unembellished meditation on the good. Consequently, there was very little hocus-pocus in it, however implausible its take on the universe, and there were virtually no conjuring tricks or any of the stage patter to go with them. Indeed, there was no priestly caste to perform tricks or indulge in patter. There was no ritual to speak of at all, now I come to think of it – not so much as a Christmas or Easter service, not even the exchange of marriage vows, let alone any nonsense about eating the flesh of Jesus of Nazareth or drinking his blood, symbolically or in any other way. There was no Mother's Union, either, or mission to save souls (in point of fact, no belief in souls at all in the traditional sense), there were no fundraising drives, no coffee mornings, film nights or even Sunday School picnics. All it offered to do, to give it its due, was to light the way towards truth (of a rather sensational kind, I must say – only a Hindu or Buddhist would not be scandalised). Paradoxically, there was something vaguely Voltairean about the whole enterprise, I tend to think now: you observe, you come up with a hypothesis about the nature of reality, you put it to the test, you talk and write about it and . . . that's basically it – with a few rousing hymns thrown in to remind you of your Christian roots.

Well, that's just not enough for most people.

Let's face it, without jewelled crosses and men in medieval dress waving censers about, religion doesn't really wash. We can get truth free in any public library any day of the week, we can google it whenever we like from any point on the globe, nobody needs religion in order to know the truth. After beginning to fly apart in the Enlightenment, religion and truth finally broke off all relations in the mid-nineteenth century. What you want from a *religion* is not truth, particularly of the private, Protestant kind that I favour, but all the garish trappings and tribal dancing. Why did I ever imagine that truth and religion could be brought back together again? What you want is precisely ritual, mystery, hocus-pocus and those ventriloquists in fancy dress, those shamans of suburbia, the clergy. Without all that – without the mummery and legerdemain, the campery and po-faced costume drama – it's just a lot of rather dodgy storytelling.

Yes, organised religion cramps the imagination, but the masses don't want imagination, they want familiar folk tales, maypole dancing and sorcery. They want Eleusis, they want Rome, they want blood sacrifice, they want Hindu temples (all much of a muchness to me), where moral behaviour is of less importance than the show. Unless you're Scottish (which my adoptive mother was), what you want from religion is fireworks and sumptuousness, the full tutti-frutti, over-the-top camp display at a gold-lamé-loincloth level. You want the impossible to be threaded back into the everyday, the sacred back into the profane, the pure into the impure, you want the loss of self annulled once and for all, and the self turned into everything. For this you need tricksters and buffoons. You need religion. You need jiggery-pokery. Or at least the masses do. I'm not talking about spirituality, I'm talking about religion, which I suspect these days is spirituality gone rotten.

The last thing on earth you want from a religion is any relevance to daily life. The trouble with my religion was that it tried to be relevant – supremely relevant. Nobody wants that. What was it that the village priest (whatever his name was – Angus, Anselm, something beginning with A) in Hilary Mantel's novel *Fludd* said? I think he was talking to his bishop. Irrelevance, he says, is surely what his flock comes to church *for* in the first place. They get relevance at home and they don't much like it. He vows to remain totally irrelevant – 'supremely bloody irrelevant' – for the sake of his parishioners and the salvation of their souls (in which he does not believe). The early Mantel is a joy. I am rather in the mood to dip into another. How embarrassing it is when churchmen try to say something relevant after a massacre or earthquake. Leave relevance to the rescue services. What the victims want is comfortingly irrelevant codswallop.

Any religion worth its salt marries people, too. Religion exists, after all, to act out the fears and beliefs, however irrational, of the tribe – that's what it's for. What could be more tribal than marriage? People will believe any kind of humbug at all if you agree to marry them while intoning it. My religion didn't act out anything. When I got married, I had to do it in an Anglican church, intoning the usual beloved banalities.

In addition to rituals, dressing up, theatre, irrelevance and marriage, you also want miracles. We didn't do miracles. You want resurrections, virgin births, flying monkeys, whatever you can come up with, really, but we pooh-poohed the whole idea of the supernatural. If something happens, however extraordinary (and unforgettable things did), it's natural.

And, above all, you want some things to be condemned as sinful, you want a whole range of delicious things you can't help craving to do frequently, such as committing adultery in your heart, not to mention in your bedroom, to be banned. The Biblical deity behaves like a grumpy headmaster in the sky, begrudging you

112

almost anything that would give pleasure. Foolishly, while looking askance at many things (too many things), and having no time for headmasters in the sky, we took the view that sinning was akin to making an error: if you insisted that $2 + 2 = 5$, you'd just have to live with the consequences until you got it right.

No wonder the steam's gone right out of it. And out of me, too, I suppose.

I still find sects appealing, I must say, even if their teachings are quite frankly hogwash. You only have to mention the Nestorians, for example, and my pulse quickens. Chinese Turkestan, for instance, since it's been wafting in and out of my mind today, was seething with Nestorians a millennium and a half ago. Outlawed in the Catholic West like so much else, the Nestorian church found sanctuary in the oases of the Silk Road. The archaeologist (or pillager, as the Chinese describe him) Aurel Stein, for instance, found myriads of Nestorian manuscripts hidden away in the Caves of the Thousand Buddhas in the Gobi desert, while Marco Polo tripped over Nestorians wherever he went in Western China. Where are they now? And what about Zoroastrians? Hardly a Zoroastrian to be found anywhere on the planet these days. The Manicheans, too, who also left traces in Chinese Turkestan, have been totally exterminated. When Candide (speaking of Voltaire) encounters one (his name is Martin) on the ship to Bordeaux,

113

he exclaims, 'You're having me on! There are no longer Manicheans in the world!' That was in seventeen-something.

What a sect is and what a conquering ideology is surely depends on the where and the when of it all, doesn't it? In Kashgar, for instance (to return to Chinese Turkestan for a moment), that smelly nodal point on the Silk Road where the Pamirs meet the Himalayas, there once lived (at the British Consulate, a Protestant bastion) a much-loved Dutch priest called Father Hendricks, who died after twenty years or more of missionary work, having converted just one Chinese boot-maker to Catholicism in two decades. At the time of his death he was no longer on speaking terms with the one other Catholic in the town, a cantankerous Pole. In Kashgar Hendricks' Christianity was an outlandish sect. I'd have been tempted to join it. At this point in my life, though, I am mostly just curious to know how believers experience a universe that is not everything, one in which for them 'the facts of the world are not the end of the matter' (Wittgenstein – he always crops up eventually). However, I feel no compulsion any more to *argue the case* for this or that view. None. Over time religion usually metamorphoses into humanism. It has in my case.

Be that as it may, it was only recently that I first said to another human being 'I am an unbeliever'.

How extraordinary that it took me so long! I'm not sure if 'unbeliever' was quite the right word – I really just fail to believe in any kind of dogma – but that's the word that popped out. I am not an atheist – atheists define 'God' and declare that this entity doesn't exist. I don't believe that religious experience is simply a sign of temporal lobe epilepsy. Trying to be an atheist strikes me as a real fool's errand, as foolish as hunting the snark, an endeavour that can end very badly indeed, we might recall, if the snark we're hot on the trail of is a boojum, in which case, like the baker in Lewis Carroll's poem, we might 'softly and suddenly vanish away, and never be met with again'. We have been warned.

At least (I can comfort myself here in death's anteroom) I have contemplated religious interpretations of the universe. At least I have given belief a go. '*Non-croyant*? A non-believer? *Moi?*' a young man I ran into a few years back in the Cathédrale Saint-Pierre in Montpellier said to me, his (sea-green) eyes wide with incredulity. 'Certainly not. That would imply that I'd given belief some thought.' I felt at the time, especially in Montpellier, that this was a case of missed opportunity.

The day I first said 'I am an unbeliever' I was walking down the hill in the warm desert air from the ancient Christian monastery of Mar Musa, north of Damascus. (I'm rather taken with monasteries, or at least the idea of them: their austere, cloistered beauty, that illusion of sanctity made flesh. We don't have them here where I come from.) I'd travelled for hours through the brown, rocky wilderness to get there. There was nothing wherever you looked: just yellowy brown rocks and plastic bags. Yellowy brown itself, Mar Musa is perched high up at the end of a completely silent, empty, yellowy brown gorge like a miniature fortress, not a tree or blade of grass in sight. From a distance it looked scarcely real. For a while, as I climbed the path up the side of the gorge towards it, completely alone, encountering nobody, nothing, not even a lizard, the monastery seemed no closer. And then all of a sudden there it was, just a few paces away. Not a mirage, but still not managing to look completely real, as if the dimension it existed in and my own had not yet quite dovetailed.

Now, Deir Mar Musa, or the monastery of St Moses the Abyssinian, is one of those historic Christian sites in Syria that everyone adopts a special expression of reverence to talk about, even Muslims. It's so old and so remote that when you mention its name a hush falls. It was established over fifteen centuries ago (I speak in round figures – the distant past is misty tonight), although the luminously beautiful small church attached to it was built much later, just before the first crusade. It's tiny, this church, with the intimacy of a private sanctuary, although high-ceilinged and covered in layers of brilliantly glowing frescoes of saints . . . haloes everywhere, I remember, Ezekiel in his chariot, a jigsaw of reds and pinks and blues . . . I knelt alone on the carpeted floor in the half-light of the candles and drank it all in.

The miracle is that, although hardly flourishing, *it is still functioning*. To this day a small and remarkably noisy clutch of monks and nuns of various denominations lives there, praying (I presume), studying (there's a library) and performing their accustomed rituals. To my immense disappointment, after kneeling in the church and then talking for a while to a very busy, worldly monk outside in the sun, I felt nothing, not even numb. I had a cup of tea on the roof, looked out over the yellowy-brown emptiness of the valley, shimmering in the heat, where Moses the Abyssinian had once been a hermit, and felt nothing at all. The monks I encountered seemed to me preoccupied with being monks, high on the fabulous theatre of being a monk in this higgledy-piggledy warren of ancient Syrian holiness. Something struck me as missing – again, I'd call it 'love' if I had to give it a name. There was passion and busyness and sanctity and learning, but I felt no love, not even in the wall-paintings, not in the monks or the other visitors – especially not in the other visitors, who mostly seemed to be German and intent on demonstrating the robustness of their faith to anyone who crossed their path. It's a wishy-washy thing to say, I suppose ('I felt no love'), but I don't know how else to put it: as I was later to find in Hindu temples, the material paraphernalia of somebody's faith, however ancient or finely executed, don't ever really touch me unless I have some sense of the love these things were spun from and are still bathed in.

At nearby Maalula, for instance, where I'd dropped in to see the shrine of St Thecla earlier in the day, I also felt nothing. It was intriguing to be in a village where everybody still spoke Aramaic, the language Jesus spoke, even sitting around in the local pizza parlour or waiting for the bus, a cigarette dangling from the lips – I love this sort of thing: the man across the room from me, talking to his neighbour, probably only saying, 'And then I said . . . and then he said . . . Anyway, what did *you* pay, if you don't mind my asking?' or something just as banal. For me, it is instant time-travel: I start leaping generations on the spot, back, back, back I go, and before you can blink I'm in Nazareth ordering a table from young Jesus, son of Joseph ('Perhaps something in red sandalwood, sir?' he asks – not exactly the sweetest-natured carpenter in town, but smart, everyone agrees he's smart). However, in Maalula, when I looked at the gorge supposedly gouged out of the rock by a miraculous bolt of lightning so that Thecla could escape her pagan pursuers, or when I contemplated her tomb or the cave she is said to have lived out her pious life in, I was unmoved. I waited quietly to be moved, not even taking photographs, but was not.

It was all so quintessentially Syrian, really: a dark and violent tale of sex and religion. (Did Syrians feel no passion for anything apart from sex and religion in some guise or other? After just a few days there, I began to wonder. I don't mean the sexual act itself so much as all the things that orchestrate it and grow out of it – family, for instance.) By all accounts Thecla was an unusual young woman: the daughter of a local Macedonian prince, she was converted to Christianity by Paul himself. Abruptly convinced of the advantages of remaining a virgin, she upped and fled her noble suitor, incurring the wrath of both her family and, quite understandably, her betrothed, who conspired amongst themselves first to burn her to death and then to let wild animals loose to tear her body to pieces. They didn't muck about in those days – insults to the patriarchy were taken very seriously. Who knows what Thecla herself, if she ever existed (not even the Catholic Church now thinks she did), was like? You sense great force of character, don't you. Courage, certainly, eccentricity verging on lunacy, perhaps, with just a touch of narcissism. However, in the extravagant trappings of her cult I feel no love. No wonder that originally, in the face of the tawdry explosion of idolatry and priestly pomp that the Christians revelled in, the Muslims wanted to clean out the stables once and for all. I couldn't be more sympathetic, but, unsurprisingly, it didn't work – not here, at any rate. Human beings adore idolatry, priestly pomp and the incantations of the sorcerers, that's the problem. They crave pageantry and the display of power. They hunger for magnificence. And why not? Without these things life for almost everyone on the planet would be unbearable.

Anyway, a little later, after wandering around the monastery of Mar Musa for a while – which is not, I hasten to add, given over to magnificence, but is austere, its small church many-hued like a dream, and calming, but not opulent – nodding and smiling and sighing and then stopping to sip tea, I set off again, alone in the hot silence, back down the path to the car park far below. And that's when I ran into a portly middle-aged Englishman toiling up the path towards me.

'Good afternoon,' he said with one of those marvellously expensive English accents you mostly hear nowadays on television programs about restoring English manor houses.

'Hullo,' I said. We both took the opportunity to lean back against the rock face for a moment to draw breath.

'So is it worth the climb?'

'Yes, definitely worth the climb,' I assured him. 'But I may not be the best person to ask.'

'Why's that?'

'Well,' I heard myself saying for the first time in my life, '*I am not a believer.*'

'Nor am I,' he said quite matter-of-factly. Oddly enough, I'd thought he might be a clergyman. 'Gave it all up when I was nine. Faith lingered on for a while like a nagging cough, but belief cleared up early on. But that has nothing to do with why we're here, does it?'

I can't remember what I said in reply, but I do remember catching myself wondering why exactly I *was* there. Perhaps in part to provoke this kind of exchange. 'Have you been to Santiago de Compostela?' he asked.

'No,' I said. 'I've never been on any kind of pilgrimage.'

'I walked the whole way from Pamplona once, when I was young.'

'Really?'

'Yes. I had the time of my life in Spain, I must say. Might give it another go one of these days – do the French bit, for example.'

'But why?'

He took so long to answer, looking out across the hot rockiness of the gorge, that I began to wonder if he'd heard the question. 'Well, I suppose I like to feel linked in to something . . . yes, I suppose that's what it is. It's an illusion, of course, in my situation and at my age, but I suppose that's why I do it. Linked in. It's probably why

121

I started learning Greek last year, too.' He guffawed. 'Even more pointless than walking to Compostela. But I'm having the time of my life with that as well. Know any Greek?'

'No,' I said. 'Some French . . .'

'Not the same thing at all,' he said. 'Everybody knows French.' He mopped his forehead with an enormous handkerchief. 'Better get moving, I suppose. Anything to drink once you get there?'

'Tea.'

'Just the ticket. Well, nice to chat! Safe journey!' And off he trudged to link himself back in to whatever he found at the top. The Byzantines, presumably.

Syria. I lie here in Darlinghurst staring at the sky, slowly floating back up from Syria. *'Nurse! Nurse! Nurse! Nurse! Nurse!'*

If it's layers you're looking for, there's nowhere on earth more layered than Syria. Talk about ganglions of history! Talk about overlapping grids! ('Shut the fuck up, you crazy cow!' someone shouts – not me, it definitely wasn't me this time. There's a brief lull.) For instance, on my second day in Damascus, at the Azem Palace, I saw a real palanquin or *mahmal*, as it's called in Arabic. It is the first, or at least quite possibly the first, certainly one of the earliest, palanquins to go on the *hajj*. (The museum attendant's whispered English was almost indecipherable.) Traditionally, he murmured huskily, any marauder worth his salt swooped first on the jewel-encrusted palanquin borne by the camel at the head of the procession because it was inside this gaudy contraption up the front that the most exalted travellers sat – pashas and sultans and emirs and so on – nervously guarding treasures destined for Mecca. A towering, pyramid-shaped structure like a pavilion at some medieval jousting match, this almost mythical palanquin straddles a life-sized wooden camel in this eighteenth-century palace in the heart of the old city. Spiralling back through the epochs, I stood there staring at it for quite a long time in the half-dark, spellbound, tumbling around dazed inside the centuries, willing it to come to life and bear me off through the palace gates, the souk, the city, out into the tawny, dry Syrian hills and finally the desert – as my driver did the next day when we went to Maalula and Mar Musa.

In Damascus, though, you can burrow back far beyond *hajj* caravans and palanquins and Bedouin raiders. I remember when I got back from the monastery, sitting in an outdoor café on the Street Called Straight drinking a banana milkshake, just where this illustrious street, whose name I've known since I was about four, passes beneath a Roman arch. Kilims, copperware and cashews were dancing before my eyes (and nose) from my stroll up the street towards the arch in the late afternoon sun. This was the same street that Paul, still blind

'Brother Saul,' Ananias
said to him *'the Lord, even
Jesus, that appeared unto
thee in the way as thou
camest, hath sent me, that
thou mightest receive thy
sight, and be filled with the
Holy Ghost.'*

Acts 9: 17–19

from the light he'd seen three days before, had ridden along with his companions, perhaps through the arch in front of me, on his way to the house of Judas, where God had told Ananias to come and find him. And Paul looked up at him when he got to Judas's house, somewhere nearby, nobody knew exactly where, and immediately saw him – 'there fell from his eyes as it had been scales' – just there somewhere, a stone's throw from where I was sitting. And he arose and was baptised. Then on they went to the house of Ananias – I could've popped around there forthwith, if I'd felt like it, when I'd finished my banana milkshake. It was just a few blocks along the street to the east and then round to the left – no distance at all. Hobart, by comparison – any Australian city, for that matter – feels a little thin.

'Nurse! Nurse! Nurse! Nurse! Nurse! Nurse!'

The intriguing thing about Syria, though, is that you can be funnelled upwards in its vortex into the future just as surely as you can be sucked down it into the past. Obviously you can be sucked down into the past. In Apamea, for instance, wandering alone down the colonnaded avenue that Mark Antony and

Cleopatra were once carried along in their covered litter, you can feel yourself sinking back through the centuries as you leave the touts and other tourists behind – of course you can. (Stan is looking at me very oddly. Did I just say 'Apamea' aloud?) You can practically smell the elephants as you head north along the rutted thoroughfare (they famously bred war elephants here, as well as the finest stallions). A dwarf selling peanuts pops out from behind a pillar to sweet-talk me into making a small purchase. Is he perhaps a grinning wraith? A hobgoblin? Did he watch Antony and Cleopatra pass? The heat is savage. My thoughts are woolly.

If you have the imagination for it, though, in Apamea you can sink down well past the Romans, centuries past the fluted columns, all the way to Alexander, to the Persians, to the Babylonians, to the Hittites . . . in fact, in the museum in nearby Hama (where I was also completely alone, the lights snapping on and off as I moved from room to room) you can hurtle back past the Hittites and their hieroglyphs (late Bronze Age – almost yesterday) to the Neanderthals, or even, if you like, to *homo erectus*, who was pottering about around Hama hundreds of thousands of years before the Neanderthals so much as made it out of Africa. I'm surprised the local mullahs allow this kind of affront to Koranic teachings about our descent from Adam.

Anyway, in Syria the layered past is almost commonplace, you can, as I say, also fall upwards into the future there.

One day, leaving Mar Musa, Damascus and Hama far behind in the west, I found myself in the museum in Palmyra, which is in the desert further east towards the Euphrates. Palmyra was once the very hub of the Silk Road that spanned the planet. It grew fat on taxing caravans: you can still see a list of the taxes levied carved into a stone tablet near the agora; you can still sit (eerily alone, if you pick your moment) surveying the stony skeleton of its magnificence, the colonnades, baths, theatre, marketplace, temples, senate. China came to Tangiers on camels through Palmyra, Rome reached Chang'an on camels through Palmyra. I rode through its empty streets on a camel myself. Then, standing in the temple of Baal (so vast it makes St Peter's in Rome look like a pimple), I was suddenly at the crossroads of my world, the Canton-to-Cadiz world that fashioned me (made Europe Europe). I could feel its east–west mesh of silky filaments begin to wheel in a billowing cloud around me and then spin. I've never felt quite so umbilical. All times were turning into one. To tell you the truth, I was still wobbling when I got to the museum back in town. And that's where I began to tumble upwards.

It started when I saw the tiny tear bottles, each one a glass tear in itself – that's when the complexion of my days in Syria changed. Now, death was everywhere in Syria – the whole country in a sense was a funerary tower stacked with bodies – but for some reason that I don't understand, it was the widows' tear bottles that afternoon in the museum in Palmyra that first 'triggered grief' in me. (That's what I wrote in my diary that night. I only keep diaries when I travel. I never miss a day. And I do reread them.) On the wall beside the tiny tear bottles is a poem. I remember only one line from it: 'You are a tear in the blood of the desert.' Whoever wrote that line had probably seen thousands butchered amongst the sand dunes and rocks of the desert, yet wept for the loss of a single beloved. We do. That's why it's touching.

From this point on, my Syrian diary starts to record a deepening awareness of how others must see me ('a thin, ageing man, perhaps even an old man', 'already a spectre'), especially in Syria, where on the streets as you stroll about everyone you see strikes you as young and full of sap. Its remaining pages are coloured by a growing anguish at having to leave my 'single beloved' forever when I die, a profound grief that I can't share even with him – I say that at some point. It's not the eternal nothingness, you see, but the leave-taking, the parting until the end of time from the being my life buzzes around like a bee around a hive – 'my home, *my heart'* (I wrote), that stings my throat with tears. It's a kind of *angoisse des gares* on an all-encompassing scale. (It doesn't work in English, this phrase about the heartbreak of saying farewell at railway stations – how curious.) The grief, I wrote in my cramped room at the Orient Hotel that afternoon, is connected to the loss of religious belief, which I felt quite acutely in Palmyra, faced with a whole pageant of half-forgotten gods, their cavalcade now not just thin but shabby, no more than a few icons and musicians shuffling past – Baal, Baal-shamin, Zeus, the Christian god . . .

At twilight, under a warm moon, from high up in the citadel outside the city, I looked back down on Palmyra. It had gone from yellowy brown to a rosy mauve.

A few days later, back in Damascus, I wrote, 'I do understand that this is a holiday from real life, that in a week real life will start again back home, and that I will start going slowly downhill until the end. I do understand this. "Discovering myself" and looking at Neolithic flintstones and then lying about in a luxury hotel-room reading a Sebastian Faulkes novel is not life, I know that – it's palliative care . . . *I'm just taking a break from time here.'*

The writing itself grows ragged. Then, I remember, I got my washing back from the hotel laundry with only one handkerchief missing – and felt 'much more positive'. Well, you do. There's something embarrassingly fickle about cosmic angst.

The night before leaving Damascus for home, though, the 'grief' became worse. 'It's unbearable,' I wrote. 'How *can* it be borne? I was so at peace. But time is starting up again. I am not afraid of death, I am full of grief. There is no help for it. Reincarnation would be a nightmare, paradise a bore. I just don't want to say goodbye forever.' But I will. Everyone does. Most of us have our little stratagems. I once had a friend in Montreal who came to the airport to say goodbye forever. '*A demain*,' she said. See you tomorrow. Bright smile. A wave. And off she strode, not looking back. What is my ploy, I wonder?

I left Syria for home the next day and time indeed resumed. Last week the moment to farewell '*my heart*' forever did indeed announce itself again. I *will* go, but for now I'm enjoying a Hindu moment: when I asked a Hindu friend recently if Hindus believed in an afterlife, he said, 'You're having it.' Wouldn't it be marvellous if that were true! The trouble with Asian mumbo jumbo, though, as opposed to our own, is that it always sounds so pleased with itself.

It's late now, here on the tenth floor. I'm misting over. Did I drift off? I lie staring out of the window at the starless sky. '*Nurse! Nurse! Nurse! Nurse! Nurse! Nurse!*' Extraordinary to think, as I've been doing off and on today, that across the road from where I'm lying and around the corner, or down the street to the right, or up the street to the left, or just over the rise to the west where the old prison stands, lie half the great crossroads of my life! Yes, out there it's my Chinese Turkestan. It was not five minutes' walk away from where I'm lying, at the end of the war, in that hospital they've since pulled down, that I was born (cross-eyed), causing infinite anguish to my unmarried mother, from whom I was smartly 'stolen', as she claimed, to be brought up as a lower-North Shore Jones. ('Smith!' a woman crowed when she saw me in a café in Kings Cross not so long ago. 'I knew you when you were Robert Smith! And if you don't mind my saying so, I didn't like that last book of yours, either, the one about that Frenchman set in Tunisia.' She leant in close. 'I loathe paedophilia, and winning the Nobel Prize doesn't excuse it.')

Across the bridge, on the edge of a wooded gully that was seething, I imagined as a child, with frogs and snakes, I led my Jones-life. We had almost no visitors, but we did have a piano, a magical radio-set with words like MOSCOW, VLADIVOSTOK, TOKYO and SANTIAGO written on its dial. We had dogs and some-times we had boarders to help make ends meet – such as the voluminous, heavily powdered Plymouth Brethren lady named Australia Deed who liked to sit me on her knee and tell me sweet-smelling, powdery things about

God. It was not a *happy* childhood (at least in the happy-go-lucky sense), although it wasn't unhappy, either; it was a dissatisfied, *thickly woven* childhood, intensely lived and full of love.

Looking back – well, not *really* looking back because I can't remember any of it – I feel as if I was a character removed from a family saga in which I wasn't wanted (at least by the main characters), to be inserted, glaring crossly, into another kind of storyline altogether (hardly a family saga, the Jones narrative) where wanted is exactly what I was. I've never felt particularly born, after all – I've always felt invented. Even now I feel largely thought-up. (But by whom?) Am I in reality here at all? (I mean, is there an *I* here?)

According to the calendar, if I *am* here, it's been for less than a week. Now there's a floating signifier if ever there was one: 'week'. 'Day' is round and whole, endless like a ball, but 'week' is just flim-flam – it doesn't mean anything at all. 'Week' is such an absurd word that I laugh out loud at the thought of it. The Korean looks across at me in alarm. I try to smile at him reassuringly. I even briefly wave, but I see quickly that waving was a mistake. He's convinced now that he's been cooped up with a loon.

Days, I'll stick with days. All the same, it's sometimes quite difficult, I must say, very late at night, especially if you wake from sleep and can't remember who you are, and time seems to have no beat, nothing to mark its passage, no rhythm at all, exactly like a measureless dirge, leaving you feeling oddly marooned with no hope of rescue . . . it is quite difficult, as I say, at such moments, to hold on to the bright daytime notion of the well-shaped, hopeful day.

∼

The head of the Deir Mar Musa community was expelled from Syria a year or so after my visit. In 2012 gunmen attacked the monastery three times, stealing whatever they could, although no monks or nuns were harmed. Rebels also destroyed the monastery of St Sergius and almost all the churches in Maalula in 2013, killing or driving out most of the Christian inhabitants. The town has since been recaptured by government forces.

10

Sunday

By the time the Peruvian nurse with the single eyebrow brings me my breakfast tray, I am wide awake and quietly enjoying the rain. A wet Sunday morning – perfect. The city beyond my window this morning has a fish-belly look to it, glistening and grey. Grey is such an underrated colour, it seems to me: from a snowy fluffiness to a playful pearliness, from mauvish smokiness to a brutal charcoal, from a feathery dove-grey to something far more lowering, more leaden, grey is infinite in its permutations. I consider it in all its wintry, drizzly, Sunday morning silveriness.

Where is Peter at this moment, I wonder? Just waking up at home? In Battery Point it's almost time for the bells of St George's to start pealing, annoying all the unbelievers. Unlike the cathedral bells in town, they always sound faintly apologetic, these parish bells behind our house, as if they know their tolling is futile. Or is he at the airport, perhaps, glum with apprehension? Peter. To say I 'love' Peter is to miss the point. We *continue* each other, that's what we do. He's not another me, I am violin to his cello.

It was in the street below this window here on a Sunday afternoon in high summer – this very street, but further north, well past St John's church and the Top of the Town hotel, up where the terrace houses start and nowadays backpackers, being young and open to adventure, hang about in slightly scruffy hostels and cafés – that I first met Peter half a lifetime ago. (It seems sometimes, as I lie here, that my whole youth played out on the other side of the glass ten floors down. It didn't really – I was young in many places – but it's certainly full of nodal points down there.)

He'd answered my little bit of cheeky puffery amongst the personal ads in the January issue of *Campaign* magazine (long since deceased). I must go to the library one day, I really must, and get that issue out of the stacks and find that ad, see what I wrote, see what piqued his interest enough in the muggy Sydney heat to make him think to himself: 'Okay, I'll give this one a go as well.' I lie for a few moments thinking of all those 'lean, straight-acting, versatile, hung' young men in the early '80s, looking for an 'attractive professional guy' (or Christian bodybuilder or bi surfer or sometimes anyone, really, into leather – but no fats or fems or Asians) for 'friendship or more', unaware of the tide of death about to wash over them – as it washed over me, although here I am, still flapping about on the surface between surges, refusing to drown. At the very least, if not dead, they'll be ageing now, as I am, if not downright elderly. What could be more dispiriting than gay personal ads from 1982? Still, I'd be intrigued to know what I put. I suspect it might strike me now as trying a bit too hard – well, I was desperate. I do know that the key word in the ad, the one that got Peter sitting down to chew thoughtfully on his biro and then send off his perky reply, was 'Mediterranean' – so much for my less tangible qualities or cultural interests.

Anyway, within days the postman had pushed his bushy-tailed note through the slot in my front door a few streets away in Paddington. All I remember about it is that Peter claimed to enjoy reading everything 'from Dante to the back of Weeties packets'. There was no photo. These days it's 'No face pic no reply' to narrow the field and save time, but in those days the first step was a step in the dark. And when the lights came on, it could be a shock. Still, I rang the number he gave me, took immediately to the voice – not deep, not resonant exactly, but, as I've said, willowy – and agreed to lunch. And now, half a lifetime later, almost within cooee of his flat in that terrace on Victoria Street, here I lie, waiting for the same voice. Which reminds me: where is he?

A few weeks later, on the third Sunday in January, I got off the bus at the stop outside this hospital, just out of sight around to the right in Burton Street, and headed off down Victoria Street past St John's, past Una's, where I used to fancy the goulash, past the Top of the Town, past the Coca-Cola sign, on towards the terrace house he shared beside the steps down to Woolloo-mooloo. He was standing on his balcony, as he later confessed, high up where

SYDNEY – Guy slim young thirties dark Mediterranean looks, intellectual, cultivated, but emotional, loving, interested theatre, seeks good looking outgoing thinker under 35, fun but sensitive. Very sincere.

Photo helpful . . .
BOX 73027

I would not be likely to look, to watch me approach, just to be on the safe side – after all, you never knew with personal ads in those days: the world, and particularly this square mile of it, was full of fetishists and depraved madmen bent on living out their freakish fantasies in the privacy of your own home. I speak from experience. You didn't want to open your front door to someone you'd understood would be an 'easy-going clean-shaven muso with swimmer's build' to find instead, for instance, a giant frog with an erection on your doormat – or worse. Who knew what sort of crazed sex fiend might be inside the frog suit?

Apparently I passed muster – at least I was invited in for a spot of ratatouille in ramekins up in his attic, and three decades later we're still together – indeed, not just together, but, as I say, you can hardly tell these days where one ends and the other begins: it's a kind of infinite dovetailing, a kind of bliss. He did wonder aloud later if shorts and thongs were the ideal choice for Sunday lunch in my case, so I didn't wear shorts or thongs again for twenty years. Well, in Tasmania, where I now live, it doesn't matter what you wear. I could wear shorts and thongs to a symphony concert and nobody would blink an eye. In Tasmania there is no parade (any more than there is in Iceland, presumably, or Nova Scotia) because everyone already knows everyone for what they are. Needless to say, however, without performance there can be little eros. In ten years there, while I have seen some evidence of sex, I've never caught the faintest whiff of eros in Tasmania. The hunger may be there, but without performance it doesn't turn into eros. Without eros what you wear is of little account. It's quite refreshing in its way, like a holiday in Scotland.

What Peter did for me over the weeks that followed was what that tram conductor in Alexandria did for E. M. Forster in 1917: he quickly turned a down-at-heel, seedy, rather commonplace city, in Forster's words, into 'the whole world'. That's what happens when you first fall in love. (Or become infatuated, for that matter, but this wasn't an infatuation.)

Is 'fall in love' the right expression for what happened to us? That makes it sound so soppily romantic. At no point did either of us *turn to syrup*, as the Russians say. (What a delicious word it is, too! I roll it across my lips and tongue and say it aloud: *'ras-SIROP-ilis'*. And then I think of other Russian words for ending up in tiny, sloppy pieces from sheer tenderness. What a language!) It wasn't one of those sudden, incandescent fusions of the body and the spirit that can knock you right off your feet, either – PSSHH! a flash of searing heat and light and you're 'in love'. ('How romantic!' everyone coos.) Nor was it simply an erotic adventure.

Romance no doubt has its place, as does the erotic adventure, for that matter – in novels, for instance, at the cinema, in Broadway musicals and amongst teen-agers clumping at bus-stops after school (or so I imagine – I really can't remember clearly back that far, and in any case things have probably changed with mobile phones). But neither Peter nor I are naturally roman-tic in the traditional sense – and it's a long tradition,

I know. Only the other day I heard someone on the radio reading out an ancient Egyptian love poem found on a scrap of papyrus – or had it been scratched on a piece of pottery? – from that famous rubbish dump in Deir el-Medina in the Valley of the Kings. Some three thousand years ago an Egyptian girl said or sang something like this to the young man courting her:

Your voice makes my limbs feel so young again!
Fat mixed with honey!

And he replied, in his voice like pomegranate wine:

And I, 'though enraptured, am not drinking beer!
To my eyes your limbs have been moistened with
cinnamon oil.

Or something along those lines. Those limbs gleaming with fat and honey, those oiled limbs scented with cinnamon have stayed vividly in my mind. Yes, it's been going on for an awfully long time. It didn't begin with the troubadors, who are usually the ones blamed for inventing it.

How poetic romantic love is, how unashamedly literary! Even those ancient Egyptians wrote a poem. No sooner does the emotional shilly-shallying get going, with its stop-start exchange of anxieties about

139

intimate feelings, than you find yourself having a stab at telling a romantic story about yourself. Romantic love is often barely sexual at all when it first strikes, except very late at night and very early in the morning. Being both well into our thirties and badly wounded the summer we met, neither Peter nor I had much enthusiasm, as I remember, for either shilly-shallying or weaving romantic storylines about a future life together. We'd already had our 'first loves' and now got straight down to what I'd call ordinary old loving: the heart. Yes, right from the beginning it was an affair of the heart. The heart is so much bigger than just the body or the emotions.

I've always chortled over a line from the opening of Turgenev's *First Love*. (A little masterpiece, that novella – a masterpiece because you've never quite finished reading it.) Three friends in their forties are sitting around after dinner late at night with a cigar and, no doubt, a snifter of cognac. It's decided that they'll each recount the story of their 'first love'. The story that sweeps us up with such immense power is told by the third man, but the first to speak, Sergei Nikolayevich, a 'round little man' with a plump, fair-skinned face, says, 'I had no first love, I began without further ado with the second.' What he means is that the first (and last) time he *fell* in love was with his nanny at the age of six and nobody wants to hear about that kind of 'first love'. In later life, we take it, he simply loved – not the same thing at all. Nothing after the age of six was a first love. (The host doesn't admit to ever falling in love: he simply 'came to love' the woman he'd already married – these were the days of arranged marriages.) In much the same spirit, I think that Peter and I simply loved. We'd already had our first (and second and third) loves. 'It's not Hollywood,' I would say to friends who wanted to know, 'but at this point in life perhaps that's better.'

Stan is giving me odd looks over the top of the *Daily Telegraph*. Have I started talking to myself again?

One thing that homosexuals all over the West were doing with panache by the time Peter and I met was demonstrating to the wider world that the most intimate, the most intensely loving, even the most long-lasting relationships need not be 'romantic' or lead to marriage – could be, but didn't have to be. Perhaps this is why we're both nonplussed by the current passion amongst some gay men and women to get married. Why on earth would you do that? To be 'equal'? I don't think so. I think they also want it because getting married is thought of as 'romantic'. But marriage isn't romantic – weddings might be, but marriage isn't. Do these people just want a big fat wedding? Then what? The one marvellous thing about being homosexual in the West over the past few decades (and there are plenty of things that have not been marvellous about it at all) is that you have been free to love and be loved – for a season, forever, deeply, sexually, asexually, emotionally, faithfully, promiscuously, wildly, gently, in a couple, a threesome, a foursome, however it suits you – without getting married. Now, on top of all the other things that make life difficult, in a growing number of countries homosexuals are also being threatened with marriage and its discontents. I get the whiff of humbug here. In fact, I am beginning to feel quite agitated about it all. When the young man with startlingly green eyes and skin like polished teak beside my bed says, 'Good morning, my name is Mahmud. I hear you are an interesting case. Could I ask you some questions?' I say no.

'I'd really appreciate it, sir,' he says. 'I'm from Bangladesh.'

'Chittagong?'

'How did you know that, sir?'

'I'm psychic.' And I can be, too, but it's unpredictable. I'm really just playing up. I examine this sprucely suited young student with interest. An awkward silence ensues. 'Alright,' I say. His crimson silk tie has undone me. It is spectacular in the early morning light. 'Come back tomorrow. Today I am a little delicate.' I should have said 'a little over-excited', but 'delicate' will do.

Mahmud flashes me a heartbreaking smile and disappears. I study the empty space he leaves behind. It's stuffed with flowers, there are whole banks of bottles, buckets and vases full of flowers – roses, lilies, camellias, gladioli – I lie surrounded by fragrant clouds of pinks and mauves and yellows and greens. I'm sure that Stan, and possibly even Ziggy, suspect there's something not quite manly about all these flowers. In this country, there is something not quite manly about being ill in the first place – especially about being a basket case. Why is this?

Since the subject has raised its head – and here I start crossing and uncrossing my feet in agitation – for a time, as I recall, homosexuals were proud of being different. Right outside this window here in Darlinghurst, between where I'm lying and those walls of glass to the west, they once wrote novels and plays about being different. They lived the lives of sexual aristocrats, not pillars of suburbia, grabbing life by the throat with a shout and a flourish before it strangled them for being as different as they were. Now the streets spread out below me are swarming with men and women who demand the right to be common. They can't wait to be monogamously married, with children, to husbands and wives, just like all the other couples in the street. Why? Why this rush back to a middle-American fantasy from the 1950s? Do they imagine it will at last give them the right to hold hands in Target? What will they demand the right to do next? Join the army? I snort rather wetly and set off a sneezing fit.

At root, I tell the cocky vase of gerberas in the corner, marriage is a legal arrangement designed to keep breeding couples and their progeny in manageable units for their own protection and the convenience of the state. But the state doesn't need marriage to manage us any more. A year or two ago, for example, when the government department responsible for pensions was about to change its rules on same-sex couples, I asked my consultant at the local office if I should mention my partner of thirty years in the forms I was filling in. 'But you do not have a partner,' she said with the sort of smile you reserve for people who only speak Urdu. 'You will acquire a partner at midnight on the thirtieth of June. Your payments will be substantially reduced accordingly.' And so they were – immediately. After making the most intimate inquiries into how Peter and I live (including sleeping arrangements), the state concluded that I was as good as 'married' and punished me accordingly.

Is that the rattle of the tea-trolley I can hear further up the corridor? I'd kill for a cup of tea just at the moment. What's taking her so long? And what's taking Peter so long?

If it's important to this couple or that to exchange vows in the sight of God, then nobody is stopping them – God, Allah, Osiris, whoever your invisible friend in the sky is, take your pick. The Pope might not cooperate, nor your local mullah, but someone in a frock in the Yellow Pages almost certainly will. You want to dress up in a dinner suit to pledge everlasting fidelity? Go for it! (The Egyptians, by the way, it now occurs to me, didn't 'marry' at all – they just moved in together and started having children. Yet their society was one of the most stable in the history of civilisations. *Think about it!*) Dress up, don't dress up, pledge, don't pledge – it's doubtful God or Allah or Hanuman the Monkey God will give a fig either way. After all, over the centuries all these gods have sat stolidly without lifting a finger through earthquakes, plagues, wars, the mass slaughter of innocents and the extinction of animal species by the million. Why would they give a toss about what name you use for the agreement you have with your partner?

Yes, yes, if gays want to marry each other, they should have the right to. You want your life to look like a Doris Day movie from 1952? It's your birthright. (A little way down the track, if you want to have *two* husbands or wives, or even three or four, why shouldn't you have that as well?) You want a church wedding with swelling organ music and confetti? How dare some narrow-minded clergyman deny you this! You want to be shackled to just one sexual partner from now until the day you die, like a Bangladeshi child bride? It's your natural entitlement. *Prego! Je vous en prie!*

'Yes, please, and make it strong,' I say when the trolley comes clattering up to my bedside. 'With two biscuits.'

One thing I do remember putting in that ad in *Campaign* was 'Interested theatre'. At the time I wrote it I was working in an amateur capacity with the edgy new Griffin Theatre Company. It's still there, tucked in behind the shops opposite the Top of the Town. It's still called the Griffin Theatre Company, too, and still likes to think of itself as edgy. I wonder if the actors duck into Una's for goulash and coffee during breaks from rehearsals as we did.

To this day I can vividly picture the set of the first play I worked on there: Joe Orton's one-acter *The Ruffian on the Stair*. Pure mischief, that play! A little gamey for contemporary tastes, probably, but in the late '70s nobody turned a hair. We did lunchtime performances, too, at the Stables: forty minutes of incest, homosexuality, prostitution, murder and the British working class at its seediest, and then off our audience would go, back to work or home to water the vegie patch, with a smile on their faces. My job was to hide behind the back wall of the set (the scenery flat) for most of the play and then, just before the end, when the gun was fired, supposedly hitting the fish-bowl, I had to smash the bowl from behind with an iron rod through a hole in the wall, letting the water, together with the goldfish I'd carved from a piece of carrot, spill out onto the floor. This was my big moment, this was theatre, this was infinitely more exciting than teaching Russian literature to a roomful of listless adolescents. I loved it. I had no interest in acting, no desire to strut the boards, I just wanted to be part of the entourage, one of the illusionists on the other side of the curtain – not that there was any curtain at our theatre, ours was theatre-in-the-round. It still is at the Stables. Who was the killjoy who came up with the idea of theatre-in-the-round?

As a small boy I'd done what lots of small boys did before television: I'd built theatre stages out of shoe-boxes – and they'd all had curtains. I would wind back the curtains to reveal the plasticine figures I'd moulded and stuck to the bottom of the shoebox. Hardly *Annie Get Your Gun* or *Quo Vadis*, which were knocking our socks off at the cinema at around the same time, but that was the whole point about the stage: it was an enchanted space. Boring once I'd opened and closed the curtain a few times, but definitely enchanted.

Until the next-door neighbours started building a garage down the side of their house, this was as far as I got theatrically. (A garage! In our street!) Excited by having this timber platform jutting out above the sloping back lawn, the kids next door and I wrote a play (something about pirates, I seem to remember, something we'd got the idea for from comics or the radio, something with weapons). Finally, one Saturday afternoon, we strung up a curtain made of sheets across one side of the wooden shell, coerced the rest of the street into buying tickets and then, brandishing cardboard swords (I do remember the swords, still smelling of paint), we strutted our stuff. The bodies piled up, the curtain was pulled back across, and we all joined the audience for orange cordial and cake on the back lawn.

As a rule on a Saturday afternoon we went 'up the street to the pictures' at the Rio (the 'R Ten' Dad called it, always up for a bit of wordplay), where we would eat Jaffas and ice-creams while watching black-and-white cowboy films as well as the occasional Hollywood spectacular such as *Singin' in the Rain* or *The Robe* in Technicolor and CinemaScope through drifts of blue smoke. Going to the pictures was almost unbearably thrilling, and the Rio smelt intoxicatingly of perfume, Craven A and children who had not yet had their bath, but it was not an enchanted space; our neighbours' half-built garage, on the other hand, for all its limitations, was. For ten minutes, thanks to a few bed-sheets draped over ropes, the denizens of our street found themselves plunged into a fantasy world they'd never have believed they could stumble across on a Saturday afternoon, outwardly like any other, down the side at number 67. Thanks to those bed-sheets, like Alice down the rabbit-hole, they'd fallen through a rip in the gauzy tissue of time – and for just one shilling, too, including the cordial and cake.

As a teenager I revelled in the illumined crimson curtains we stared at in a kind of excited rapture, waiting for the play to begin, when I went to the theatre with my mother. We always sat up in the gods, my mother and I, facing this vast wall of glowing velvet, above and below us, imagining in our naïveté that waiting for the curtain to go up was a precious part of a ceremony granting us some sort of communion with the realm we could not yet see. I watched Brecht's *Caucasian Chalk Circle* from up there, I remember, as well as *Who's Afraid of Virginia Woolf?* and *A Taste of Honey* – well, perhaps not always in the gods and not every time with my mother, but that's my memory. When you lived in the sort of street in the sort of suburb we did in those postwar years, if you had a jot of feeling for what my mother called 'the finer things', the theatre was a portal linking you to existences unimaginable in Austin Street, Lane Cove.

I'm still enchanted by curtains, believe it or not; I still hanker after curtains, wings and hidden places where, at the very least, bewitchment, if not blacker arts, are hatched. I don't want it to be plain that there is no realm apart. A play is not a circus performance. A play is not even a ballet, either, although it's hard to put your finger on the difference. We did also go to the ballet,

I had not been to the theatre for twenty years and I had no intention of going again now. It was not even a question of liking or disliking the theatre. The important thing was the pleasure that came from not being interested in the theatre . . . Not being interested in the theatre means a whole area of life and culture means nothing to me: there are entire sections of listings magazines that I don't need to consult, vast areas of conversation I don't need to take part in, great wads of cash that I don't need to consider parting with. It is bliss, not being interested in the theatre. Not being interested in the theatre provides me with more happiness than all the things I am interested in put together . . . Oh, bliss of indifference!

Geoff Dyer, *Out of Sheer Rage* (1997)

my mother and I (*Petrushka, Peter and the Wolf, Pineapple Poll, The Nutcracker*) and were entranced, ensorcelled and spellbound . . . but mostly entertained. A play, though, should feel like a visitation.

That mischievous English writer Geoff Dyer insists that he's bored by the theatre – isn't interested in stories or plots in general, but especially in the form of plays – and how marvellously liberating this is for him – so much time and money saved, so much *keeping up* he doesn't need to do. (I feel the same way about America.) It's in his painstakingly plotted account of trying to write a study of D. H. Lawrence and failing utterly. Somebody invites him to see a play Lawrence wrote and he says that he hasn't been to the theatre for half a lifetime and has no intention of going now.

This sort of naughty-boy posturing is amusing in a well-educated, grown man, as it was in the even better-educated Samuel Johnson, who did at least write a play himself – just one and it only had nine performances, but he did once write a play. His wife, I seem to remember, thought very highly of it. When a couple of friends called upon him one evening – Goldsmith and Boswell, I think – the conversation turned to the theatre and they chided him over his lack of interest in the latest plays London was abuzz with. He defends himself pithily, being Johnson. I used to enjoy the theatre, he retorts, but I don't any more. That's what happens. I am not *obliged* to keep up taking pleasure in it. At this point in my life I shall do as I please.

GOLDSMITH: 'I think, Mr Johnson, you don't go near the theatres now. You give yourself no more concern about a new play, than if you had never had anything to do with the stage.'

JOHNSON. 'Why, Sir, our tastes greatly alter. The lad does not care for the child's rattle, and the old man does not care for the young man's whore.'

GOLDSMITH. 'Nay, Sir, but your Muse was not a whore.'

JOHNSON. 'Sir, I do not think she was. But as we advance in the journey of life, we drop some of the things which have pleased us; whether it be that we are fatigued and don't choose to carry so many things any farther, or that we find other things which we like better.'

BOSWELL. 'But, Sir, why don't you give us something in some other way?'

GOLDSMITH. 'Ay, Sir, we have a claim upon you.'

JOHNSON. 'No, Sir, *I am not obliged to do any more. No man is obliged to do as much as he can do. A man is to have part of his life to himself. If a soldier has fought a good many campaigns, he is not to be blamed if he retires to ease and tranquillity. A physician, who has practised long in a great city, may be excused if he retires to a small town, and takes less practice. Now, Sir, the good I can do by my conversation bears the same proportion to the good I can do by my writings, that the practice of a physician, retired to a small town, does to his practice in a great city.'*
BOSWELL. *'But I wonder, Sir, you have not more pleasure in writing than in not writing.'*
JOHNSON. *'Sir, you MAY wonder.'*

Not just a naughty fifty-something-ish boy, Johnson was also proving himself to be a wise man. Dyer, I can't help thinking, although a writer I take great pleasure in reading, was missing the point about theatre – or at least a point. What is it, exactly? (I study the gerberas. I actually dislike gerberas.) It has to do with enchantment, I think. But what is enchantment? I'm trying to find the words to describe it.

It's not mere magic, which can be rather a tawdry affair, like special effects in modern movies. People *say* 'Oh, it was magic!', 'It's been a magical evening!' and so on, but what they mean is 'really nice'. Magic is a trick. It can be astounding, but not enchanting.

Goa floats into my mind. I was sitting in the foyer

152

of a hotel in Goa with my head in *Kim*, waiting to be picked up and taken to the airport. All of a sudden, half an hour or so before the driver was due to arrive, a towering beanpole of a young man with a ravishing smile appeared beside me. 'Goodness me!' I said. 'What white teeth you have!'

'Yes, Mr Robert,' he said, 'they run in the family. My name is Fayaz. Do you have a few minutes? I'd like to show you some tricks.'

'Yes, Fayaz,' I said, 'I do. Thirty, in fact. And tricks would be just the ticket.'

He led me off across courtyards and around various infinity pools until we got to the Business Centre. He was, he told me in his rapid-fire, faultless English, ushering me inside, the hotel magician, employed to amuse the children. 'I saw you in the wee hours, sitting all alone, drinking your tea. I thought to myself: this gentleman might like to see my tricks.'

'Oh, I would,' I said. 'Anything you'd like to show me.'

He shut the door firmly, took out a pack of cards, shuffled it and told me to pick any one. I did. 'You've chosen the queen of hearts!'

I turned it over. It was.

'I wonder who the queen of *your* heart is!' he said. He then snapped the cards back together again, shuffled, fanned them and asked, 'What takes your fancy this time, Mr Robert? The king of hearts?'

Cheeky. I drew out a card. It was the king of hearts. I gasped. He smiled.

'And this time?' he asked, offering me a half-moon of shiny cards again.

'Well, we may as well go for the jack of hearts,' I said, 'don't you think?' I chose. It was indeed the jack of hearts.

'This time the ace,' he said, smiling toothily. He splayed his cards, I drew one out, I turned it over. It was the ace of hearts.

'But how do you do it, Fayaz?' I croaked, dumbfounded. 'Magic doesn't exist.'

'No,' he said, nodding loosely in that disarming Indian way, 'magic does not exist.'

'And do all those hearts mean anything?'

'Nothing at all. Nothing means anything. It's all a trick.'

And then he took a coin out of my ear, found an egg in my pocket and rolled back his shirt-sleeve to show me that he was wearing my watch. I was speechless with astonishment. Putting the watch back on my wrist, he whispered in my ear, 'But goodness gracious me! What's that you've got in your back pocket?' It was, of course, the joker. 'I'll have to keep my eye on you, Mr Robert,' he said. 'Who knows what else you might be making off with? Should we take a look?' Was he about to show me a few even more eye-opening examples of his light-fingeredness? What time was it? Then somebody started rattling at the door and we had to stop.

His flim-flam had flabbergasted and delighted me, it had bamboozled and beguiled me, but it had not enchanted me. Enchantment is not a trick.

Strangely enough, since India has just been in my thoughts again, I'm convinced that it has something to do with *darshan*, especially in the theatre. During the performance of a play – a performance that is happening now, tonight, here, unrepeatably, just for you – the actors' gaze, or at least their presence, interlocks with yours, like Kali's with mine in Kuala Lumpur. Interlocking can't happen at the cinema – it can't even happen on live television. A play is dangerous, too – it can go disastrously wrong, it can slew off the rails and kill, if not someone, then at least something, and this is mesmerising, like a car race. A play scoops you up into its moment in the dark, it strives to seduce you, it makes love to you, it wants something of you, it can't be itself without you. I don't have that sense about any other art form. It was during my years at the Stables Theatre, where I did everything from painting the scenery to serving the coffee downstairs in the interval, from chairing meetings to filling out grant applications, that I learnt something about how good theatre is made – not enough, that goes without saying, but something.

A well-made play, I believe, keeps people in their seats, wide awake and waiting; a well-made play has them flocking back after the interval, eager for the transformative moment they're convinced is coming, much as a good book does, in its fashion. But, from the writer's point of view, there's a difference.

I am still a little shocked, for instance, by the way a theatre piece you've written can just thumb its nose at you, put its hat on and take itself out for a walk with its friends – and it behaves differently every time it goes out, too, depending on who it meets up with. You can tell it how to behave (some scripts are littered with instructions such as 'laughs quietly' and 'takes aim with a sneer'), but in the end it does what it likes: a respectable tragedy starts cavorting in public like a farce, while a comedy, in certain company, turns into a kitchen-sink drama. It's much harder for a book to misbehave like this. A book may be misunderstood, it may mean something slightly different to each reader, and so, theoretically, there may be as many 'versions' of your novel, biography or memoir as there are readers, but only theoretically – it's still yours, what it means is not infinitely malleable: *Emma* simply cannot be construed as a novel about voodoo.

A play, it seems to me, exists in some other way entirely, more like a musical composition or a conversation: only in performance by other people. Even when

I was writing my play, it often felt as if characters were saying to me, 'Sorry, I just wouldn't say that – that's you, not me.' At times I felt like Shirley MacLaine channelling beings from another dimension – whatever dimension it is, in my case, that Turgenev and those he loved have ended up in. I've never felt like that while writing anything else. Even before anyone got hold of it – readers, a director, actors – I could hear other voices. It was intoxicating.

Well, it's my big week, this week. Come Friday night, I'm on! It looks as if I'm going to miss the performance itself, marooned instead, as the lights go down in the theatre, flat on my back amongst all these vases of flowers up on the tenth floor of St Vincent's. At this stage, I still can't hobble to the bathroom. It doesn't matter. It's still my big week.

Those shoeboxes . . . now I come to think of it, in effect I'm lying here in the cardiothoracic ward at St Vincent's amongst all those flowers because of playing with those shoeboxes sixty years or more ago. That led directly to dressing up as a pirate in the neighbours' backyard, which in its turn led on to those evenings in the gods at various theatres in Sydney that are no longer there, which led eventually to those nights smashing fish-bowls at the Stables just up the road in Kings Cross, which is where I one night met the virtuoso director Aubrey Mellor, lover of all things Russian, together with whom I later translated several of Chekhov's masterpieces and who would one day give me the confidence to try my hand at writing my own play, the very play that I came over to Sydney to have workshopped at the National Institute of Dramatic Arts and, after keeling over, fresh off the plane, more dead than alive, will not now see performed. Aubrey is going to be there for the performance, although these days he lives in Singapore, of all places. I think about Aubrey. Such a warm man, a *floating* man . . . no, not a floating man, but a man, like Anthony, always on the point of taking wing.

To say that I'm here 'because' of the shoeboxes may be to oversimplify things – indeed, the word 'because' always oversimplifies things, doesn't it. I don't quite trust it. Yet there's clearly a connecting thread linking those shoeboxes and my bed here at St Vincent's, even if at one point it became very slender indeed, as in hindsight the threads that everything in life hangs by do. 'It hung by a thread!' we often say. Well, of course it did! What else would it have hung by? A hawser? Being chosen by the Joneses, for instance, out of the thousands who might have chosen me that March day in 1944, to be taken across the bridge to be their son, also hung by a thread – it was illegal, after all, as my mother later told me, because they were far too old, especially Tom, who was born in the 1880s. Yet the thread held.

Meeting up with Peter all those years ago also hung by a very meagre thread – castaways on desert islands have thrown messages in bottles into the sea with more hope of being rescued than I had of finding someone to love for the rest of my life when I posted off my advertisement to *Campaign*. And the calling of that ambulance manned by the paramedic with the burnished forearms hung by a thread – two thin ones, actually: first of all, against all the odds, the kind stranger with FUCK YOU on his t-shirt picked me up from where I lay slumped and stinking of faeces in the street after midnight and walked me back to my hotel – he did not pass by on the other side, as he might well have, but had compassion on me (as the King James version has it) and saved my life; and then the night porter at the hotel refused at the last moment to let me take the lift to my room, where I would have died alone within minutes, instead making me sit down in the foyer and calling an ambulance – he also did not pass by on the other side, as he might well have, but had compassion on me and saved my life. These threads were so slender as to be almost invisible, like a spider's web, yet they were as strong as steel.

I vividly remember the moment at the Stables when the theatrical thread virtually snapped. It was at a lunchtime performance of the Orton when only two people turned up to see it. The Griffin Theatre Company came within a whisker of ceasing to exist that lunchtime.

The three actors and I went on with the performance, the audience of two sat through it in silence, untouched, it would seem, by the stabs of scandalously black humour. The stench of the ludicrously failed lives on the stage wafted across the theatre and down the stairs into the deserted foyer where the four of us met afterwards to discuss the failing fortunes of the company. There was only a whisker in it, I can tell you. If one of us had so much as sneezed, the company would have folded. As it was, we kept our nerve. The Griffin Theatre Company survived, fattened and flowered. The thread held.

I smell rain. I smell wet wool. I open my eyes. It's Peter. He's back. My continuance. My wholeness. His happiness at being here again fills the room. My heart leaps.

'You flew again,' I say.

'Yes.'

'Did they tell you to?'

A pause. 'I wanted to.'

'And what about the dog?'

11

Monday

Goodness me! Ziggy's gone! Where he was there's nobody. Is it Monday? What time is it? I seem to be flickering on and off like a faulty fluorescent tube these days, although I am not the least bit concerned. I am too shallowly here this morning to feel agitated.

Not only has Ziggy vanished, I now notice (I'm having trouble focusing), but his bed has dematerialised as well. It's as if some sorcerer touched him with his magic wand while I was asleep and *poof*! he's melted away, leaving nothing behind but a square of bare linoleum. Is he dead, I wonder, or has he just gone private? He's been threatening to. Stan is still here, but is curtained off, partaking rather noisily of the Blessed Sacrament again, while the Korean in the fourth bed is blankly watching a programme about Botox on Channel 7, so I can't ask either of them what's happened.

And then I notice him by the window: the prankster himself, that is, grinning mischievously. He's cleverly turned himself into an Indian.

'Good morning!' he says. 'I hope this is not too early for you.' Too early? It's coming back to me now: he's not Indian at all, he's Bangladeshi. And what's been worrying him, of course, is not that it might be too early, but that it might be too late.

'Mahmud,' I say. 'That's a relief.' Saying his name out loud like this crystallises things. What marvellous eyebrows, by the way. The erotic possibilities of eyebrows are almost infinite. (I do hope I didn't let that slip out as well.)

'So,' he says, brushing aside my mumblings and consulting his clipboard, 'shall we get started, Mr . . . how do you pronounce your name?' I tell him.

'Is that French?'

'Yes, but I'm not.'

'I see. What family do you have?' This seems rather abrupt. How long has he been here? His tie this morning is turquoise, my favourite colour. Fingernails I'd have loved to kiss.

'None,' I say. I'm suddenly feeling much better. He looks appalled.

'None at all?'

'None.'

'No . . . ?'

'Nobody.' I mean that I'm not a link in any chain of grandparents, parents, siblings and progeny grouped around a hearth. I have no sense of a chain or a hearth.

'I'm sorry.'

Why? Please don't be, Mahmud. *Families, I hate you!* Mahmud is looking at me oddly. Have I said any of this aloud? Just in case I have, I say, 'André Gide. *Fruits of the Earth* – an early work,' and think to myself, tapping out the rhythm with my fingers, '*Foyers clos, portes renfermées* . . . Their homes closed off, doors shutting all others out . . .' Much pithier, and at the same time more poetic, in French. This interview has begun badly and it's my fault. I've travelled in Mahmud's part of the world many times and know perfectly well why he pities me. A man without family where Mahmud comes from is as good as dead. My eyes come to rest on his gleaming turquoise tie.

There are people I love deeply, naturally – just a handful, but there are some. The thing is this: I choose who I will grow close to.

No family history, then, of this type of thing? An awkward smile.

History? Well, no, not really – I mean how would I know? I'd like to help, Mahmud, I truly would – for statistical purposes, if nothing else – but I can't. The only scraps I could offer you – a cancer here, a suicide there and one death in a helicopter crash – would not be of the slightest use to you.

What were you doing at the time of the attack? It happened in the street, I understand. In Oxford Street.

Oxford Street, yes. I know what you're getting at, Mahmud. As a man without family, I am also without much shame, which could be to your advantage here. (And for the same reason, interestingly enough, I'm not very good at glee, either. Delight and joyfulness, even *jouissance* . . . but not jollity or glee.) To feel shame (or glee), you must first live in what anthropologists call a face-to-face society, you see, like an ancient Greek *polis* (or a village in Bangladesh, for that matter), or else belong to a clan or a family, or at the very least a club or coterie. You must have *mates*, you must be on a *team*, because shame is about being caught breaking someone's rules – the rules of some community or other (now, there's a word to chill the blood) – it's about being exposed. Shame is about nakedness. When you're ashamed you stare at the ground and wrap your arms around yourself defensively. I might feel *embarrassed* about being caught out misbehaving – or smoked out (even worse): tribes often gang together to smoke out rule-breakers – but, having no village, clan, family or band of mates to keep its eye on me, no community on the lookout for deviant behaviour, I do not have a strong need to look away, to cover myself up or hide who I am from the gaze of others. It's not that I don't care what people think or that I see no point in rules – naturally I do – but I feel no need to look down or cover up. Not here, not in this country. In Bangladesh I'm sure it's very different.

I remember being dumbfounded years ago when I first told a Russian friend that I was moving in with a man – Peter. Well, he's the only man I've ever moved in with. Appalled by such flagrant disregard for what was socially acceptable, she cast about for something crushing to say. 'But you'll lose everyone's respect,' she said finally. 'Nobody will . . .' – she scrabbled around for another, more wounding word, but couldn't think of one – '*respect* you any more.' There was a silence. What the fuck, I thought to myself, nonplussed, has *respect* got to do with anything? Why would I give a rat's arse about anybody's respect? Love, yes, but respect? The silence continued for a while and then I put the phone down.

Perhaps this shamelessness is what makes me 'interesting' to interview: I will look you straight in the eye and tell you *almost* anything you want to know, so long as I sense no malice.

I consider Mahmud and the silky splash of turquoise on his chest. It would be illuminating to discuss the finer points of shame and shamelessness with Mahmud, they're something he'd know all about, but this is not the moment.

Had you been having sex or using drugs before the attack?

It's thanks to this shamelessness, I am now convinced, by the way, that I was never, not even once, bullied (or 'abused') at my school just over the bridge in North Sydney, or anywhere else, for that matter, when I was growing up, despite being so obviously (what shall we call it?) different. Nothing *sportif* about me. All the same, small, scrawny and suspiciously well-spoken though I was, really from the moment I began walking and talking, and in adolescence uninterested in sexual conquests of the expected kind, the kind that validated your maleness, I had no shame, and that protected me. 'Bold' was what an older Catholic cousin of mine used to call me (disapprovingly) when I was a small boy. (I liked being thought bold. I took it she meant like Dick Tracy or Batman, whose adventures I followed avidly in comic-books on visits to the barber. Boldness was excitingly in evidence on every pectoral-laden page of the lurid *Classics Illustrated* comics as well – in *Ivanhoe*, for example, and *Quo Vadis*, which I was obsessed with when I was about seven because I'd seen the movie. When I was a boy you chose your barber for the range of comics he offered.) She also once called me 'pert'. She meant 'brazen', of course – my cousin meant that I was insolent in my Protestant defiance of her church, uncowed as I was by priests or the need to confess. The shameless have no need to confess. They might tell, but they don't confess.

I also never learnt how to 'choke off empathy' by playing sport. It's a phrase that stays with me from a remarkable essay I read not long ago on American sporting culture and its connection to child abuse. It's on the sporting field that young males 'get the hang of hatred' (an unforgettable phrase), the writer says. It's there they acquire the craving to divide the world into victors and victims that feeds the desire to abuse – and worse. I hardly appeared on the sporting field – just footled about on the edge of rugby matches once a week every winter while I was at high school because I had no choice. I never learnt the rules, never worked out what 'offside' meant, for example. In summer I used to stay at home feigning illness on Wednesdays when the school headed off to the baths for mass swimming (the very smell of the changing sheds full of wet boys made me queasy) or else I helped my father arrange the bottles in the bottle-shop he managed for a while in Balgowlah. I grew up with plenty of empathy. You can't write without empathy. (I also grew up delighting in the bottle – not in alcohol, to which I have a rather Islamic attitude, but in the bottle.)

Yet, *because I had no shame*, unlike some of my weedier schoolmates, I was not bullied, mocked (at least not openly, to my face) or subjected to physical abuse of any kind, ever. As the author of this heart-wrenching essay argues (what was his name?), you bully (and molest) boys who are not just unmanly or unsporting (he himself was molested in a Catholic boys' baseball team), but boys who will feel ashamed of being bullied, and even of being sexually molested, and be inclined to blame themselves for not staying innocent. In Christian countries you especially target boys who will feel that being abused is tantamount to committing a sin.

(Hoffman is his name, Richard Hoffman. The neurons are beginning to fire.)

In this respect being bullied and abused is like being punished for bed-wetting (which is something I've been doing all week, by the way).

Where were you when you first lost control of your bowels? On the street after the pain had started or upstairs?

In another marvellous essay, this one on bed-wetting (amongst other things) at a grotesque institution unforgettably called St Cyprian's, the author . . . he's famous, the name will come to me . . . ORWELL, George Orwell – there, you see? Still firing . . . Orwell wrote that, while it seemed to you in your innocence to be beyond your

168

control, at his school you were held to blame for wetting the bed, just as you were for homosexuality. Bed-wetting at St Cyprian's, he writes in this luminous and lethal piece, was a sin you committed without even knowing that you were committing it, or wanting to do so, or being able not to. A sin could even be something that happened *to* you (like original sin). No wonder it's in Roman Catholic and other church institutions that sexual abuse is particularly rife. No wonder Ireland reeks of it. I never had the faintest notion of sin – my version of Christianity acknowledged only truth and error. 'Sin' was not a word we ever used – that may be one of the reasons I took to that particular creed in the first place.

Orwell also singled out sport at St Cyprian's as a corrupter of youth for teaching boys that virtue consists in winning – that some deserve to win and always do, while some deserve to lose and everlastingly do; that some are simply born to bully those beneath them, to make them suffer and look foolish. On many an afternoon during football practice on the oval across the road from where I once lived in Hobart I could hear boys from the select Anglican school up the road being trained by their masters to be thugs – to crush, to kill, to fucking win. And if you had the impudence to ask these guardians of the progeny of the ruling class to tone down their violent language, you risked being threatened yourself, as we were. For that matter, millions of us – not just the Stans and Ziggys amongst us – still sit mesmerised night after night watching 'reality TV' shows such as *MasterChef*, *American Idol* and *Survivor*, brutal last-man-standing contests to find the biggest, strongest, handsomest, most popular, and sometimes even the most unscrupulous, deviously dominating men and women in the land. Even today in the public arena, virtue is still more or less synonymous with winning.

At 69 Austin Street, Lane Cove, however, where I grew up a Jones in genteel, lower-middle-class pennilessness (never poverty), life was not hierarchical, and virtue did not consist in winning, nor wickedness in losing. At our place, a short tram-ride from the city, that idea never entered anybody's head. (What makes trams so . . . what is the right word? . . . so *civil* as a means of transport?) I grew up to disapprove of all sorts of things, sometimes very strongly indeed, as young people everywhere do in their rigidly conservative way, but the St Cyprian's notion of wickedness never took root in my consciousness. I took responsibility for what I chose, but would refuse to take responsibility, sometimes with quite breathtaking impertinence, for what I did not consider I had chosen. When you are adopted, after all, almost everything in your life seems *chosen* – you choose your friends (and have no *real* given relatives), and you choose your various enthusiasms (for foreign languages, say, or in my case snowlines and little-used suburban railway stations, such as Warrawee, at which I would briefly alight on Sunday trips around the rail network with my father as if trying to make them feel wanted). Even your talents, foibles, vices and strengths seem chosen when you're adopted. Inherited characteristics don't come into it. I think I believed I'd chosen my body.

I had, after all, been chosen. Cross and cross-eyed in my hospital cot, I was chosen by Tom and Jean Jones. They thought, Tom said, that I looked as if I'd turn out to be a real little character. Or perhaps they first saw me in my cot at the Strathfield home for unmarried mothers that my mother was moved to with me – I'm not sure. Wherever it was, at least my mother held me for two weeks before I was taken from her. As we now know, babies were often forcibly removed from unmarried mothers at Crown Street the moment they were born, with the grief-stricken mothers shrieking, 'I just want to see my baby, please let me see my baby.' Sometimes, we have now been told, the girls at Crown Street were held down with a wooden restraint board while the baby was pulled away from them by force. Then they were sent home as if nothing had happened, as if they'd been away on a holiday in Terrigal for a few months (for the last twenty weeks of their pregnancy, as a rule).

It was horrific. As well as the young mothers, the brutality traumatised nurses and obstetricians for life.

The pain – where did you feel it? What was it like? How long did it last?

For me, for tiny Trevor Royal, as my unwed mother had it in mind to call me, I have to admit that being removed and taken across the bridge to Lane Cove was an unmixed blessing. Not for my mother, but for me, certainly. It was not an enchanted childhood by any means – an only child's life with middle-aged working parents can be lonely, and Lane Cove was dull. But I was astoundingly free – free from and free to: free from expectations about what I should be and free to love what I chose to love. Even today Lane Cove is hardly a throbbing cultural mecca: Nicole Kidman may well have gone to school there (the same school I went to, actually), and it might be on the right side of the bridge (the Eastern Suburbs remaining faintly louche, and anywhere else, however expensive, being out of the question), but it's a far cry from Bloomsbury or the 6th arrondissement. At that time, though, it wasn't just sleepy but curiously lifeless – the perfect place to commit a murder, as one of my mother's childhood friends from Perth declared, once safely inside the house. She only stayed one night. At some point a Chinese restaurant opened in the main street, but the Joneses didn't feel comfortable eating foreign food in a public place.

Nobody with any flair lived in Lane Cove, except for the artist Desiderius Orban and he was Hungarian. In that small brick house not far from the tram terminus, there was no music apart from what I played myself on the piano, and the only books we owned were French phrase books and grammars and a treasured *Pears' Cyclopaedia* (Tom bought a new one every year) – a dictionary, too, I'm sure, there must have been a dictionary. There was probably a *Reader's Digest* condensed book or two as well somewhere in the house, although if you wanted to read a book, you mostly borrowed it from the library. All the same, I grew up unusually free, not in an anarchic way, in quite a prim way, but free to choose. To this day, as Peter keeps remarking, I find it quite difficult, for all my gifts of empathy, to understand why anyone would choose to be a slave. Yet people do, in their millions, even to unseen masters. Being free is beyond most of us.

Of course, when I took up my particular version of Christianity (unrecognised as Christian by most Christians, and derided as dangerous humbug by all of them), I also accepted limitations on my freedom. I was joining a kind of team. As Paul explained it to the Corinthians, if you'd been a slave when the Lord called you, you were now free in the Lord, and if you'd been free when the Lord called you, you were now His slave. Is that clear? In other words, like love (and communism),

Truth frees the slave and enslaves the free. Is Mahmud free, I wonder? Or is he a slave of Allah? (He seems to be talking to me, by the way. And strangely enough, I seem to be mumbling something back.)

When I think of our house in Lane Cove all those years ago, with its backyard disappearing into the snaky bush straggling up from the gully behind and its front garden smelling of warm lantana and mown grass, one of the first things I can hear is the postman's whistle. There was the clip-clop of the baker's horse as well, of course, and the rattle of the billy as the milkman delivered the milk, but I didn't know the baker or the milkman, any more than I knew the iceman or the rag-and-bone man. The postman, though, was my friend. Every time he rested his bicycle against a fence on his way up the street to slip letters into a letterbox, he gave a short, sharp trill on his whistle – unless you were standing there waiting for him, as I often was of an afternoon, swinging on the gate under the jacaranda. 'How are you, young Robert?' he would ask. (He knew all the names of the people on his rounds, of course, as I did. And naturally he knew our dogs, as I did.) 'Now, have I got something special for you today? Let's see . . . hmmm.' And he'd rummage in his ballooning leather bag of mail. 'What's this, now? From Sweden! That's a long way away. Have you got a girlfriend in Sweden?' Or it might have been from France or West Berlin. It would be a slim, almost weightless blue envelope (stamped PAR AVION or FLYGPOST or something equally exotic) that I'd rush inside to my bedroom to tear open. Tearing open a blue envelope from Europe was a voluptuous delight, even the smell of a thin blue envelope from Europe gave me a refined kind of pleasure. What on earth did a Gothenburg flower-shop owner's daughter and an Australian schoolboy find to say to each other? Or a twelve-year-old watchmaker's son in Reims? Or, later on, a Berlin doctor's son living just yards from the thrillingly evil wall in Zehlendorf? Camphausenstrasse he lived in. I always loved the word Camphausenstrasse, I relished saying it aloud. (By the look on Mahmud's face, I fancy I have just said Camphausenstrasse aloud to him.) What do adolescent pen-friends ever find to say to each other? Do they still exist? What was it that gave us such intense pleasure? Eventually, when we were in our twenties, I visited both the grown-up French boy and the German. It wasn't a disaster but it spelt the end of the affair.

There was, I think, a sensuousness to our exchanges in those days, to our bonds with friends and neighbours (do people even have *bonds* any more?), to our connectedness. Below me on the street, when I stood at the window trailing cannulae for a moment yesterday, I could see a whole army of interconnected people interconnecting on little handheld devices as they hurried along the pavements, cut through the parrot-green park opposite, stood queuing for coffee at the rotunda and scurried across the road between the cars and ambulances. Yet they appeared to have no eyes or ears for the world surrounding them. They moved about it like bacteria under a microscope, sensually disconnected. Some of them may well have been in touch with Gothenburg, Reims and Berlin at that very instant, I know, not to mention cities and towns all over Australia, in an immediate way unimaginable to me when I was young; others were probably listening to voices beamed in not just from Melbourne or Murwillumbah, but from Milan and Montreal and Moscow, places I had to save up for years and then travel to in order to hear voices; and, since this is Darlinghurst, half of the males I was peering down at were no doubt setting up shockingly sensual, if fleeting, encounters for later in the day with bodies they'd been scrolling through on casual dating sites on these very same handheld devices. Yet, to my eyes, their feverish connectedness had an oddly disembodied, almost incorporeal quality to it. There is nobody *there* any more – or here. There's no *darshan*. Half the world looks stupefied. Intimacies are conducted at several removes and so can't be genuinely intimate, not really, not *intimate*, any more than the intimacies we believe we're having with the characters in our television sitcoms we watch nightly can be intimate. Television has got a lot to answer for: it looks like *darshan*, but it's not.

There's an almost fetishistic aspect to the scene being enacted ten stories below me every day – and all around me on the tenth floor of St Vincent's, for that matter, as well as on the ninth and eighth and every other floor of this and every other building I can see from my window: a fixation on an inanimate object with magical powers to connect you to invisible, even imaginary, beings elsewhere in the cosmos, exactly like a saint's shinbone. Is there not, as in the worshipping of such relics, a spooky kind of narcissism at play here? Is there not the whiff of people obsessively talking to themselves about themselves while pretending to adore an unseen presence? Sometimes, for instance, when a certain kind of mystic has assured me that the object of his meditation is to lose all sense of self in the allness of the deity, in the oceanic Oneness of all being, I get the uncomfortable feeling that in reality self has not been extinguished at all, but, on the contrary, has expanded to gobble up not just the yoga and meditation class I've mistakenly enrolled in, but the whole of North Hobart – in fact, with a sinister *whoosh!*, the entire island of Tasmania and, judging by the look on his face, in rapid succession the Earth, the solar system and the galaxies, from the beginning of time to its end. Suddenly and mysteriously it has all become co-extensive with a slight, pale young man from Bath Street, Battery Point. Well, I smell the same kind of rat when people talk to me about connecting.

It's possible, though, that I remember the sensuousness of my attachments all those years ago, the strange fleshiness of getting to know the world and the people in it, because, being a child, that's what I mostly did – got to know the world fleshily. Perhaps all those beetling figures ten floors down had childhoods just as sensuous as mine. Mine rustled and croaked and sang and smelt and burnt and tingled and soothed and fondled and dazzled. Even to telephone, when I was a small child in Lane Cove, meant to climb the hill in front of our house to the red telephone box at the top where, sweating behind the glass in the western sun, I would call my friends – Susan Varga, for instance, who was Hungarian, or my best friend Geoffrey, who was an Anglican – and talk until dusk for just a penny – or was it later tuppence? – about things we both loved.

In Susan's case, I was always enchanted to think that this friend I was talking to could think in Hungarian. Without even trying, she could think in a language I didn't know one word of. I bought a book on languages to see how this extraordinarily foreign tongue worked – I still have it: *The World's Chief Languages* by Mario A. Pei (George Allen & Unwin Ltd, 1949); it smells now of silverfish and ancient inkiness. (To this day, from time to time, I'll take it down and over a cup of coffee leaf through Tamil verbs or the imperative in Japanese as a kind of *amuse-bouche* for the mind.) Then I went back up the hill and rang Susan in even greater amazement. Her mind was unimaginably different from mine. The world, it turned out, was made up of people with unimaginably different minds from mine. My pleasure in this discovery was voluptuous.

A lifetime later we're still talking, Susan and I. (Geoffrey and I are still in touch as well, although more haphazardly.) We're like the two sides of an arabesque, in a way, looping out and then back again, each a mirror image of the other. The appealing thing about arabesques, surely, from the Great Mosque in Damascus to the wrought-iron grills on backstreet windows in Chittagong, where Mahmud comes from, is that you can imagine the pattern going on forever. The winding and twining *out* and the winding and twining back *in* have a dancing rhythm to them that no line of tiles or window-frame can stop. An arabesque thumbs its nose at edges. Still, after sixty years, Susan and I are probably both coming to some sort of edge. Coincidentally, in recent weeks, we've both come almost simultaneously to a very big edge indeed, but both stepped back from it, shakily, and sat down. Even in this the pattern has held.

It's marvellous the way children sense things, isn't it. When we were both nine or ten, we could already sense kindred spirits. At school just across that bridge behind Mahmud . . . *Is it still Mahmud? Are my eyes playing tricks on me?* . . . in a classroom hung with spelling charts and watercolours we'd painted ourselves, I was on the constant lookout, having no kin, eyes now well and truly uncrossed, for souls that were kindred. In some cultures there are broader notions of kinship than we have – some quite outlandish: I think the Inuit regard anyone who has had ringworm as kin – but I was more traditional: I had no real kin. Yes, I may have been free of shame, being without blood relatives, but I also felt from my earliest years, having no family, a strong need for relatedness of some other kind – in a word, for intimacy. Every child may well yearn for it, but at the outset most children find it first inside their family – indeed, many men fail to ever find it anywhere else. As I grew up, though, threatened as I was by abandonment *again* ('We're not young, you know,' my mother would say, 'we could die at any time'), I sensed early that I'd better start searching for intimate relatedness elsewhere – or rather start *choosing* intimate relatedness else-where, intimacy being created by choice. A child with little sense of a given family learns quickly to be ready to choose. You're always on the alert for signs of affec-tion. As a small boy I didn't have a word for what I craved, but that's what it was – not just someone to love, not just 'best friends', but the chance to choose intimacy. As an adult this eagerness to choose is an unappealing quality, I now think – it can look like neediness. As an adult, too, fearing isolation, you're often tempted to take the most alluring shortcut to intimacy: the shared orgasm.

And over near our classroom fish-tank there was Susan (who went on to write a book about her mother, her first book, in the very same year that I wrote a book, also my first, about my mother); in the playground there was Geoffrey from the class next door, who went on to high school with me and emailed me about something or other as recently as last week; and, now that he's dead, I can come out and admit it: at the front of the class there was also Mr Lowry, our teacher – 'sensitive', as my mother liked to call such men, and a bachelor, although I could scarcely be intimate with him. All three of us were kindred souls. And while I can't speak for the gentle Mr Lowry, Susan, Geoffrey and I all went on to lead lives with a remarkably similar shape and colouring. At nine or ten you know almost nothing about how the world works, but you can spot a kindred spirit a mile off.

Susan and Geoffrey did have kin, loving kin – mothers, fathers and sisters, mostly in the upper reaches of the North Shore, quite a long tram and train journey from where I lived. Where their gift for growing close to kindred souls, and not just members of the family, came from, I don't know. How did they know when still so young *how to attend to what matters to others*, and not just do things with them? And why did they choose to do this? Perhaps, like me, they were self-contained in that way that, paradoxically, you need to be in order to excel at intimacy. Yes, oddly enough, there's often an aloofness about the skilled practitioner of intimacy, almost an introverted quality at times, that leads to a hunger for shared emotional intensity. It's astonishingly rare, I'm quite convinced, the gift for intimacy – not just affection or friendship, but intimacy. 'Intimacy,' I say, quite distinctly, startling even myself. 'What is it, really?'

The Russians are good at tender attachments. What words do they have? I send out feelers for words. The word *zadushévny* swims into my mind. You can have a *zadushévny* friend or conversation or even secret. It's a tender although not fragile word. It has something to do with the soul (the *dush* bit), perhaps with a quality that grips the soul, or even tucks itself in behind the soul (the *za* bit). But that's not enough. I need more words. I look at Mahmud. Does Mahmud have a gift for intimacy? Mahmud will certainly have kin. In Chittagong I imagine everyone has kin. Perhaps kin will be enough for him. (It was, I know, for the mother who gave birth to me. All her intimate relations were with kin.) 'I'd quite like to go to Chittagong one day,' I tell him – if it's still him: it's hard to be sure against the mottled brightness of the morning. (What else have

I told him this morning?) And I would, too. It's not at the top of the list, to be frank, it could well turn out to be one of those places which Samuel Johnson (was it not?) said were worth seeing but not worth going to see. All the same, I'm a Silk Road man at heart, and the Ganges–Brahmaputra delta was a trading hub on the south-west branch of the Silk Road thousands of years ago. Strabo the Greek knew about the Brahmaputra delta, Roman merchants were buying and selling there when Julius Caesar was a boy – this is common knowledge, and my mind takes off like a kite in the wind at the thought of it. 'I may not, of course, be going anywhere at all,' I hear myself cackle after a pause. I clear my throat. 'But I would like to. There's a hopefulness to travel, don't you think?'

'Well, I don't know about Chittagong,' he says, 'at least for now. Let's concentrate on getting you home first.' And there it is again, that light-brown voice, that voice like smooth willow . . . Peter's voice, it's Peter, it isn't Mahmud sitting beside me at all. Whatever happened to Mahmud?

'It's you!' I say, suddenly elated. I flap my cannulae at him to show how pleased I am to see him. 'I thought you were someone else, but it's you.' I'm smiling so broadly that I'm slurring my words. 'How long have you been here, Peter?'

'Quite a while. You've been dozing.'

'Getting me home . . . Have you come to take me home?' And, being a little emotionally delicate, I shed one small salty tear.

'Not quite yet, no. One thing at a time.'

Who or what was talking to Mahmud, then, while I, or some form of me, flitted about the Lower North Shore, looking in on old friends? I suddenly feel quite Egyptian.

'What did you say?' He leans towards me. 'You feel what?'

'Quite Egyptian.' (I try to say it again, but it's surprisingly difficult to get your lips and tongue around 'quite Egyptian' when you're not yourself.) I feel as if I've split into three, the way Egyptians did when they died. Am I more or less dead myself, then? My father, Tom, a lapsed Catholic, always suspected that I was the reincarnation of an Egyptian scribe, partly because I was swarthy and had begun writing in hieroglyphs at the age of two, but also because he'd taken a fancy to Madame Blavatsky. Her predilection for things Egyptian, including threefold souls, is well established. Interestingly enough, Tom kept some of my early scribbles to show me later, and I must say there was an uncanny resemblance. Superstitious gobbledygook, the lot of it, that's beyond question, but all the same, there *was* an uncanny resemblance.

Be that as it may, the Egyptian notion of souls splitting into three at death describes with bizarre accuracy the way I feel now, this minute. Firstly, there was the *ka*, which was the life-force itself, apparently, someone's *spirit*, whatever is gone when the body is dead. But I don't think *that* is what was talking to Mahmud, even if I am in fact dead: the *ka* was not chatty, sounding to me more like the Hindus' breathy Brahman – 'spirit' and 'breath' being related concepts, after all, in many languages (well, they would be, wouldn't they – no breath and you're not there any more). *Pardon?* Oh, nothing important.

Secondly, there was the *ba,* which was the self that performed in the world, hardly spiritual at all, keen to keep indulging in all the usual bodily pleasures in the afterlife, from eating to copulating: was it perhaps my *ba* that entertained Mahmud with tales of its exploits in Oxford Street while performing as Robert? Meanwhile the third self, the *akh*, ruminated on the meaning of everything, roaming the world, or in my case this morning Darlinghurst and the Lower North Shore, like an ibis-shaped ghost.

Complete hogwash, the lot of it, clearly, utter tripe and tommyrot. Apart from anything else, I'm still breathing – only just, as it turns out, but I am.

On the other hand, in the secret language I began to flesh out as a very small boy, stimulated, perhaps, by

Susan's unfathomable Hungarian, and knowing next to nothing about the Egyptians, *Ka* was the name I dreamt up for the Great Spirit hidden (so the locals claim) in the bowels of the imaginary island where my secret language was spoken. *Is* spoken. Where to this day, by the way, a small settlement beside a turquoise volcanic lake in the centre of the island is called The Little Eye of Ka – just two words in my language, although what they are I hesitate to divulge.

Odd that the Egyptians had no word for 'religion', by the way, particularly when they spent more of their gross national product on religion (the afterlife, their gods, their temples and priests and so on) than any other nation in history. A complete waste of time, really, a waste of being alive. Or was it? Which reminds me: in this secret language of mine, I, too, have never found a word I'm happy with for 'religion'. Here I am, all but dead in a hospital bed, and I'm still trying to come up with one. At some level I can't work out what on earth 'religion' is.

'What are you looking so pleased about?' Peter asks.

I have no idea. I simply can't remember ever feeling happier than I do at this moment. Not ever. I am recollecting in tranquillity with Peter watching on. Out of chaos I am condensing, dissipating and once more spontaneously condensing over and over again. I am deeply alive. I am replete.

In the corner opposite I notice that Ziggy's back, too, large as life, as if he'd never been gone. An excellent omen, that.

'Would you like some tea?'

'Yes, please. With two biscuits.'

12

Wednesday

I think I'm seesawing up at the moment instead of down. It's an exhilarating sensation. 'You're our star patient,' the doctor from Zimbabwe said to me yesterday. She means that I've surprised them: despite everything, I seem to be rallying. I was even up to taking a walk this morning, trundling my intravenous thingummyjigs along beside me, Peter gripping my other elbow. We made it as far as the sunny lounge area near the lifts. Doesn't winter sun put a smile on your face! Just a few minutes of winter sun and your spirits soar! In little knots all around the room patients and their visitors sit in the sun, talking softly to each other, all wanting everything to be alright, you can see it in their eyes. We stood there at the window in the sun for quite a while, Peter and I, looking out across the city, hardly speaking, just remembering. The future's a bit foggy, but the past is a panorama. I can even see quite clearly what was never there.

Take, for instance, my imaginary land, the place I still spend part of each day in. Whatever sort of wonderland of memory and desire the city out there might represent, it has nothing to do with the island kingdom I conjured up when I was seven. There's no Little Eye of Ka to be found in Darlinghurst! For a start, the geometry is all wrong. No, no, I may well have lived out most of my double, quadruple, octuple lives in amongst all those sunlit towers and slabs of glass (abandoned newborn, lovestruck waif, contemplative, bohemian, thespian, wanton, voice on the radio, monk, and on and on – there have been so many), but the shabby fairyland I was looking at this morning bears no resemblance to my concocted land, to my square within a square (times seven) within a circle (inside six more circles), to my blue and gold and mauve Shambhala. None at all. Why would it? That's the whole point of invented lands: they're nothing like this one.

Shambhala. Just as the mythical Tibetan kingdom of Shambhala had a capital city beginning with the letter 'k' (Kalapa – a name I find evocative for some reason, a name with possibilities, I wish I'd thought of it), hidden away in Siberia, some say, or on the banks of the Nile, as you might expect, or the lower reaches of the Himalayas, which is quintessential Shangri-la territory, not far from where the Dalai Lama's settled, so does my Shambhala, my invented land. Needless to say, when I first dreamt it up as a small boy, out the back between the bushy chook-run at the bottom of the yard and the first line of washing, I'd never heard of Shambhala, although if you believe in karmic connections (speaking of velar plosives), that may be of little account.

I happen *not* to believe in karmic connections. Instead, I am convinced my attraction to 'k' sounds comes from *Five on Kirrin Island Again* by Enid Blyton. In Enid Blyton's Famous Five books, George has her own island to play on, together with her dog Timmy and her cousins, and it begins with a 'k'. I wanted one too – much, much bigger, of course, than Kirrin Island, one half the size of Tasmania, really, but with a ruined castle just like the one on George's island. Simple as that. And just as Kirrin Island lies off the south coast of England, my island of K lies off the south coast of Alaska.

Enid Blyton, and *Five on Kirrin Island Again* in particular, shaped me in a way no other writer or book ever did, with the possible exception of Richmal Crompton and her William stories. William also lived in rural southern England amongst the comfortably-off, come to think of it, just like George and her cousins. To be honest, some wispy, childish part of me still fantasises about living in rural southern England amongst the comfortably-off. Shakespeare colours the consciousness of every educated Australian, that goes without saying. Shakespeare's language, characters and themes are a background radiance from the time you reach high school until you die; and at university I discovered Nikolai Gogol – he infected me with his preposterous characters and outlandish language, he laughed at my dead soul; but Enid Blyton and Richmal Crompton moulded my day-to-day imagination in more profound ways than either Shakespeare or Gogol. This was mostly because of the age I was when I read them, I presume. (And why Mr Lowry had a much greater effect on who I grew up to be than any teacher I later had at high school, or even at university.) Is Harry Potter having the same effect on the young of today?

It wasn't the ubiquitous ham sandwiches and lashings of ginger beer that sculpted my view of the world, nor the cries of 'Oh blow!' when things went wrong and 'Wizard!' when they went right, nor was it the jumble sales organised by vicars' wives. (I know, I know – there never were any lashings of ginger beer, but it feels as if there were. Curiously, Lashings of Ginger Beer is now a radical lesbian burlesque collective. What does burlesque actually mean? I've never been sure.) No, it was more a question of the subtext: the idea of loyalty to your close friends no matter what, the sharing of secrets with them (an important part of growing up), and also the unusual gendering (although I wouldn't have known as a child what to call it): I was always rather taken with Julian, such a willowy yet manly youth, fair-haired and tall (like Peter, who is still quite willowy), good-natured but firm (as Peter is), with marvellously determined eyes and a strong chin . . . and his cousin George such a bossy girl, the real boy of the group ('a son to be proud of', somebody says of her) . . . and their sixteen-year-old neighbour at Kirrin, the sulky loner Martin, who has no parents, is artistic and apt to sob, just like me, really, which is, we're told, a feeble thing for a man to do. Men, as we know, are meant to enjoy *doing* things, not appreciating things of beauty for their own sake. The objects men are meant to like also have to do with doing things – golf clubs, for instance, or outboard motors. Martin's a boy, but isn't like that at all. Martin made quite an impression on me.

The Famous Five are often called right-wing racists. They might have been racists, I can't remember, but there's nothing right-wing about them in *Five on Kirrin Island Again*: the whole plot revolves around foiling the dastardly attempts of wicked men from 'big business' to destroy George's father's ingenious secret alternative to coal, coke and oil. Anyway, I forgive them their peccadilloes. I refuse to watch those cruel spoofs on their adventures, too – what are they called? *Five Go Mad in Dorset*, *Five Go Mad on Mescalin* and so on. The Famous Five were my friends.

Exploration in Blyton's world is perfectly manly and at the heart of any adventure. My love of travel has many roots, I'm sure – my voyage to Perth with my mother on the SS *Maloja* when I was six, for instance, a ship at sea being more exciting than a castle for a little boy; Tom's years at sea as a wireless operator, too – his photographs of Yokahama, Vladivostok, Hong Kong, Singapore . . . small yellowing snaps in an album I've still got . . . somewhere, it must be somewhere . . . where is it? I hope they haven't been lost. He was dashing in his white uniform, he always looked as if he was his own man in those snaps. He was never his own man at home – you aren't; he hankered after those years at sea, I think, and got a job at the Overseas Telecommunications Commission office in York Street (in the old AWA building with its fabulous conical steel tower), sending cables out across the globe. I used to miss sport on Wednesdays to be there with him, not just at the bottle shop, marvelling at the men coming in to send messages to Reykjavik, Mombasa, Santiago, Mexico City, Cairo and hundreds of other unimaginably mysterious places, not only London and New York. How exciting to be one of these men talking to Icelanders and Kenyans as if they were in the next room.

Yes, there were many sources of my love of leaving home, I can see that, but I wonder if the true source of my odd infatuation with those explorers of the Silk Road, the men who dug up buried cities in the howling wastes of High Tartary a century ago, unearthing frescoed labyrinths in the desert, vast caches of ancient Buddhist manuscripts and long-hidden hoards of silks and amulets, may have been . . . I blush to say it . . . but I can see the connection . . . the Famous Five, the first explorers I ever knew. The Swede Sven Hedin, for example, the German von Le Coq and, most illustrious of all of them, Aurel Stein, who was British to boot, even if Hungarian by birth, the discoverer of the Caves of a Thousand Buddhas in the Gobi desert: I very likely thrill to the exploits of these stupendously courageous explorers, rapacious plunderers though they were, because right at the beginning, when I was tiny and books were time-machines and windows on the wonders of the world, I read about George and Julian and the gang on faraway Kirrin Island, finding hidden treasure and fighting off their foes.

I also learnt from Enid Blyton that fun always involves a dog. (Even Aurel Stein travelled with his terrier Dash. All his terriers were called Dash.)

In a word, for little Robert Jones in Lane Cove, the plot of *Five on Kirrin Island Again* thickened in more ways than one.

Once you come up with an invented land of your own, however, you're going to need street maps, towns, railway lines and highways wending their way amongst rivers, plateaus and lakes, as well as all the other paraphernalia of this toy-train world in your head. (In *Five on Kirrin Island Again*, it now occurs to me, playing with toy railway stations and their miniature porters and guards is a perfectly respectable thing for even a grown man to do.) In other words, you'll have to come up with a specific geography for your land and you'll have to come up with names for all the things in it. You'll need a currency, too, you'll need DO NOT WALK signs, vans with the word for POLICE and AMBULANCE written on them, epitaphs on gravestones, newspaper headlines, noticeboards in front of libraries, posters outside theatres, restaurant menus . . . all of a sudden you'll need a language and a script. Then you'll want to people this landscape (the trains, the cafés, the schools, the shops, the temples, the streets – not so much the factories and the abattoirs) with locals who talk. They'll want to talk about what was and what will be and should be. They'll want to make jokes, curse, chat about the weather and make public announcements. At least, that's how it happened in my case. In no time at all this land was alive with language. As recently as this morning, sixty-odd years later, looking out at Darlinghurst, I was crafting the local word for 'seedy'. Some children might make up secret languages to play games in and to keep adults and other children in the dark. I clearly made up mine, like Adam, in order to bring my beloved invented land to life. In other words, after a while I started to need not just geographies, but also customs, a history, myths, religions, a culture with values unlike any we cherished in Lane Cove (although nothing remotely elvish, I hasten to stress) and therefore a language, one pleasing to the ear, naturally, vaguely redolent of Italian – I never went in for words like Psglqkxxk. Tolkien (since 'elvish' has come up) seems to have done it the other way around: started making up languages (fourteen in all, I seem to remember reading somewhere) and then the world in which they were spoken.

In the end, what we're all doing, we inventors of lands and languages, is refusing to accept the world as we've found it. We are utopians. When I was very small indeed, just beginning to draw town plans of the capital of my island on sheets of paper my father stole from the office, I had no need of words such as 'seedy'. My imagined land was pure. At the centre, unlike Sydney or our messy backyard, it was all square, a brightly coloured Shambhala, thought-out, purposeful, intricately designed yet basically simple, an idealised version of what I saw around me, where to my frustration there seemed to be no end to rotting, sagging fences, peeling walls, smelly laneways, chook-runs and unkempt yards. Lane Cove was no slum, but it was by no means a freshly painted toy town or the Tyrol. (I was in touch with the Tyrol through my German class at school, I had posters from the Tyrol all over my bedroom walls.)

I had a horror of 'slums' as a child, as a matter of fact, excitedly getting off the train on those Sunday circuits of suburban stations with Tom at Macdonaldtown, not far south of the wrong end of town, if we could find a train that stopped there. It was the very nadir of slumminess, as far as I was concerned, the dark heart of terraced squalor. I would quickly say to myself 'I am standing in a slum' and then jump back onto the train. I could not imagine, having been nowhere except Perth, anywhere grimier or more wretched, anywhere more in need of being made pure, than Macdonaldtown. To this very day, apparently, many of its residents pretend not to live there, claiming they live in Redfern or Erskineville or Newtown. Macdonaldtown has been made to disappear. In the old days the locals mostly worked at the ugly nearby railway workshops. I suppose they've all been turned into art spaces, have they?

In my Pure Land there was no place for railway workshops. Trains just ran. To be quite honest, there wasn't really much place for work. I could hardly walk when I first understood that pleasure of your own choosing – leisure in the best sense – was infinitely preferable to work. So, naturally enough, cities in my Pure Land were in the early days rectangular, architecturally harmonious and given over largely to leisure and culture, with just a hint of banking. The Greek agora has always appealed. (The Japanese Pure Land sect, it now strikes me in a quasi-mystical flash, had its origin in Chinese Turkestan. Is this a serendipitous coincidence or am I being stalked by Chinese Turkestan? Perhaps after my Egyptian phase I was reincarnated as a Buddhist in Chinese Turkestan. I really must look into this Japanese Pure Land business one of these days.)

As the years went by, though, my land, along with its language, became less a little boy's utopian fantasy of leisured perfection, screening off for hours at a time a reality that was beneath him, than a setting in which to let a growing range of competing, even contradictory, fantasies play out (political, for the most part). I was growing up. If your fantasies aren't contradictory, how can you take a bearing on who you are? And just as my land now had its Macdonaldtowns, railway workshops and parks best not entered at night, improprieties and solecisms began to crop up in my language. From being obsessively regular at its birth and almost preternaturally well-behaved, like some correcting mirror held up to the warped world around me, in adolescence it now thrived – indeed, throve – on breaking the rules, on warping the world anew. It became dystopian. Verbs went unpredictably haywire, with multiplying moods and persons, nouns started sprouting declensions quirkier than anything I'd come across in Russian (which is a complete nightmare in its own right in this regard), and the grammatical complexities of something as outwardly simple as 'Is that the lunch trolley I can hear?' would boggle even my mind, although this boggled mind of mine was after all the same mind that had come up with the complexities in the first place.

Some adolescents may have spent their leisure hours lost in the realms of space exploration or sporting feats, some may have gone to sleep at night trying to nut out problems of evolutionary biology or compos-ing rock songs in their heads. I did this. I am not, of course, ashamed of my toy world with its toy language, but I am fully conscious of how . . . what word should I choose? . . . how *frivolous* by comparison, how utterly footling, verging on tinpot, my fantasy life has been since I was six. All the same, it's been a window onto my own mind. It's been where I can safely play at not being me, and this is quite a useful skill to have in understanding other people.

Ever since Hildegard of Bingen concocted her private language for communing directly with God some 800 years ago, sages (Bacon, Descartes and Leibniz, to name just three, but modern savants are still doing it and posting their systems on the internet) have played with the idea that with a little tweaking from a perfect language – that is, a tongue both *con*cise and *pre*cise – reality itself might emerge from the clouds of ignorance and stupidity. A tempting idea, but wrong. These perfect languages can't be spoken, can't be lived. In fact, the more irregular and corrupt my language became, the easier it was to talk to myself in it.

At some point many of the linguistic miniature village builders amongst us have thought to themselves: before Babel, all the world was one – and so it can be again. Speak Esperanto (Volapük, Solresol, whatever) and humanity can be reunited: we can be one again. But do we want to be one? Not really, not these days. These days we like diversity, we're suspicious of oneness. God never thought 'being one' was a good idea for humanity, as the Bible explains, getting very peevish indeed when He first clapped eyes on 'Babel' (the 'Gate of God'), which in its insolence mankind had built to celebrate its oneness. The point is that we like being scattered upon the face of the Earth, speaking a profusion of confused languages. We find disorder creative. Linguists write books about the need to save from extinction languages spoken by the tiniest pieces in the mosaic of humanity.

After all, there's always English if an Eskimo wants to speak to a Zulu.

Anyway, who wants to save the world these days? The world is a lost cause. What at least some of us want to do in the twenty-first century is *express our many-sided selves*, even if we turn out to be the only audience for the performance. More particularly, we love to fantasise about being many kinds of people who in reality we can never be: a communist, say, in my case, or a pioneering prison warden, a minor prince in a barouche, an acrobat, a millionaire, a hippie, triplet, father of four or famous concert pianist, a hot-air balloonist, Buddhist abbot, Armenian priest, maharaja, unaligned president of a tropical paradise, even an eighteenth-century French count – there's no end to the possibilities. I do it by imagining that I'm a character in a multitude of stories set in my invented land. (I read novels for the same reason. That's why I like to read novels about people I am not, in lands that are not mine.)

I suspect that most contemporary secret languages are uncommunicated, undisclosed affairs, as mine has always been, private stabs at being creative by bringing into being a world imagined in its entirety. When the Creator Himself did this, He reportedly began with language, like Tolkien. 'In the beginning was the Word, and the Word was with God and the word was God.' Basically, though, I have only the vaguest notion of what this could mean – I know what the exegetes say it means, but I'm little the wiser, really. All the same, I like it. Language is usually thought of as a kind of pact between its speakers. If there's only one speaker, who is the pact between? Different sides to the self, I suppose.

Yet my language does speak to me of a kind of orderliness and of origins. When you feel you've been invented rather than born, both patterning and origins take on special significance for you. Indeed, ever since I was a little boy I've had a passion for pigeonholing – for grammar, cataloguing, colour-coordinating and, yes, quite simply for putting things in bottles and boxes. Especially boxes, anything to do with boxes: I am besotted with boxes, I have a weakness for all of them – *papier-mâché* boxes, lacquered or carved, wooden boxes, shoeboxes (as I've explained), cardboard boxes of any kind, to be honest: for miniature boxes, even matchboxes, as well as wine cartons and plastic storage boxes, for coffers, trunks and chests of wood. I have also had a passion since early childhood for headwaters, so to speak, for distant, common origins, deep roots I know we all share (not having anything shallower to play with) – hence my infatuation with the Silk Road (which is not just a tangled web of lines on a map of the world, but something that courses through my very being, from glowing nub to glowing nub, joining what's Western about me to what is Eastern, joining Hull to

Honshu) and hence my passion for proto-Indo-European, the tongue my ancestors spoke (as did most of my readers' forebears) on the grasslands north of the Black Sea and around the lower Volga about five thousand years ago or possibly thirty thousand years ago on the Don, nobody knows. Spookily, nowadays I can hear stories told in it on my computer.

The Black Sea, the Don, the lower Volga – that reminds me: yesterday afternoon, just as the sun went down and that cabbagy smell I like so much began to waft through the ward, Karen dropped in to see me, without Anthony this time. 'He's feeling a bit ragged today,' she said. I didn't know whether she meant he was beginning to flag or was having a nervous breakdown. We both smiled in an understanding sort of way.

After a week or more of being Russian at the rehearsals out at NIDA, she looked as if she'd just blown in from the steppes.

'You're looking very Russian today,' I said.

'And what does that mean?'

'I can't tell you, Karen, but I know it when I see it.' Or was it just the smell of the cabbage?

It's not really a look, it's more the slightly wabi-sabi feel that Russians give off – or used to give off (your better class of Russian, that is, not the crowds milling in the metro) – in *my* day. Is that why the Japanese were so attracted to them – to Chekhov, Dostoyevsky and the rest? The Japanese used to lap them up. (As a matter of fact, speaking of wabi-sabi, I was feeling just a touch impermanent, imperfect and even a little asymmetrical myself yesterday by the late afternoon. There's something soul-destroying about the tedium in a hospital ward: the tedium is laced with menace, the monotony broken now and again by moments of excitement. The odour of dying gerberas added a touch of melancholy to the scene, and one-legged Stan's invocations to his deity the usual note of utter futility. At one point I began to hiccup from panic.)

Anyway, whatever Karen was, she certainly wasn't French. Which is odd because in several pivotal scenes in the play she's not Russian at all: she's Turgenev's paramour, his lifelong love, his passion, his inamorata, Pauline Viardot (actors have to double up these days – this is not Moscow in the 1960s). Come to think of it, though, Pauline Viardot wasn't French either, she was Spanish, she was just married to a Frenchman and lived in France. Yesterday Karen didn't have that rigorous snobbishness of the French. I've been accused of rigorous snobbishness myself. It must be genetic. Be that as it may, I'm sure Karen can carry Madame Viardot off with panache as well. How I'd *love* to see her do it!

Anyway, yesterday afternoon, when she swept into the ward, aglow with having been somebody she actually isn't all day, I felt the world that my play is set in float in with her. It's been so hard to hold onto that world these past days – to the museum nobody much ever visited, for instance, or the nameless provincial town it's partly set in . . .

BORIS:
It's just a bog, this town.
VASSÍLY:
A what?
BORIS:
A bog. We're stuck in this town like stumps in a bog.
VASSÍLY:
A bog?
BORIS:
Yes, a great big stinking bog. Are you going deaf now as well?

Its garrulous townsfolk have drifted out of earshot, even old Vassíly, my modern-day madman (and therefore the only truly happy man in the play), along with the ghosts of Turgenev and Viardot in his head – I've lost my grip on it all. Even with Anthony popping in to see me whenever he could, it's misted over. Or I've misted over. But yesterday I could step into it again now that Karen was there, I could move in and out of it for half an hour or so, I could be in two worlds at once.

'Not long to go now!'

'Just a few more days!' she smiled. 'We're nearly there – not quite, but we'll make it.'

I won't, of course – not to the theatre, I mean. But that's not what's important. 'So how is it shaping up?' I tried to sound laid-back about it.

'Well, it's different every day,' she said, choosing her words carefully. 'As a good play should be in the beginning. Some lines aren't working, some lines still have no *roots* when we say them, do you know what I mean?'

Yes, I knew what she meant: some things in the play have no history here. We talked about some of the things that they'd all decided would have to be changed (chopped, shortened, moved around, made clearer) – it was their play, too, after all. 'The hardest thing for us to get a handle on is whether it's a comedy or . . . well, not a tragedy, it's hardly a tragedy, is it, nobody dies, not even the cat, but . . .'

'I don't think it's either of those things. It's really just very sad,' I said, casting my eye around the darkening ward while I looked for the right word, my eyes alighting on Stan, Ziggy, the Korean, the bloody gerberas, 'with here and there a dash of farce.'

13

Friday night

They come to me from time to time, you see. Oh, yes, they come and talk to me, here in the museum. People think I'm daft – 'You're off your rocker,' young Boris says to me, Boris from Interactive Services, 'you're a . . . psycho' – but they do. When the time is right. When everything is quiet and . . .
(Pause.)

PING! It's Vassily speaking. It's just gone eight o'clock, the lights have gone down and, alone on the stage, he's begun to speak. In a flash I have come to and am almost piercingly present.

I call out aloud, 'It's Friday night!' Somehow or other, all those bluish scraps of days and yellow-black shards of night, all those scattered beads of time that came flickeringly to life inside me for an instant here, an hour there, are trailing behind me now like a necklace: Sunday, Monday, Tuesday, Wednesday, day, night, day, night . . . and now it's Friday night, my second here, although I can't recall the first. Yes, Friday night, not just another patch of darkness streaked with light, but Friday night, my Friday night, my big night, the night I came here for.

At one minute past eight, a few miles away to the south, John Turnbull will be sitting on a chair delivering Vassily's opening lines to my very first audience since that play about pirates in the neighbours' backyard a whole lifetime ago. Is he getting it right? Has he captured the old duffer, roots and all?

'They come and talk to me.' Vassily *sees* things, he really does. When the time is right, and everything is quiet, they come to him – if they know he's waiting for them. They're not ghosts, why call them ghosts? And they're not fairies at the bottom of the garden, either. They're his soulmates from the past, that's what they are. He can see them as clearly as I can see the night nurse bringing Stan his bedpan, and he can talk to them. They only come once the unbelievers have all left the museum, though. At two minutes past eight not all the unbelievers have yet left.

DÁRYA GAVRÍLOVNA (*crossing the stage hurriedly*): Vassíly Iványch! Can you lock up tonight? I'm late for my yoga class. And I haven't even begun to pack for Odessa. Oh, God, look at the time!

I can hear Karen say these lines so distinctly. I can hear the click of her heels. She'll get these lines exactly right, Karen will. Full of vim, brisk, anxious, kind of sexy.

VASSÍLY:
Of course, Dárya Gavrílovna. I'm in no hurry. I'm never in a hurry. Where would I be hurrying off to? Who's waiting for *me* to get home – apart from my cat, Mr Pushkin? An absolute gentleman, by the way, Mr Pushkin is. Loves Tchaikovsky. (*Pause.*)

It's three minutes past eight now and they're well and truly off and running! Yes, in that theatre on Anzac Parade I'm finally *on*! It's hardly Shaftesbury Avenue, I know. It's not even off-off-Broadway, it's a *reading*, for God's sake, a reading on a platform in a rehearsal space (it's not even a theatre) at the drama school in front of a few dozen well-wishers at best. All the same, as I speak (through Boris or Vassily or Pauline Viardot – whoever

I'm ventriloquising through) I'm being heard, that's the thing. After all, it's been such a joy to me, writing this play, like a half-hidden affair that blossoms just when you were thinking you were past it. Years it's taken me, on and off, years of clandestine scribbling and rewriting to get it into shape.

I do hope it's not a complete dud, this play of mine, my one and only. Has anyone at all (apart from Peter, Scott and Aubrey Mellor) turned up to see it? I do hope it doesn't prove to be my 'greatest failure', as someone called Samuel Johnson's one and only play *Irene*. In fact, come to think of it, it was Johnson himself who said that. His stunning flop has been haunting me ever since last weekend when Johnson came to mind. And he'd spent almost twenty-five years writing his play, too – not quite half a lifetime, but almost. I've spent less than half a lifetime on *A Mad Affair*, but many years all the same.

Why on earth did I write it? I'm beginning to wonder. I do remember being fascinated decades ago by that mysterious hour in the train that Turgenev spent with the actress Marya Savina and what he wrote about it, and much later in life I do recall resolving never again to confuse infatuation with love (as we all do because so few words spring to mind to describe what we've been going through). But that was a long time ago and doesn't really explain why I decided to write a play about it all. It's the performance, isn't it? It's the hunger for sorcery; I am in love with the idea of performance in front of a live audience – you don't get that when you write books. But more than that: it's the *darshan*, that's what it is, it's the electrifying sense of seeing at the moment of being seen. I wanted to try my hand at conjuring up *darshan*.

The inspiration for my doddering Russian museum attendant comes straight from Paris. One day at the Musée Carnavalet in Paris, with the first two or three versions of the play already under my belt, I noticed as if for the first time in my life the uniformed attendants scattered throughout the building amongst the paintings, the *objets d'art*, the period furniture and the archaeological remains. Russian museums are haunted by legions of cantankerous attendants, there's one in every doorway. You'd think I'd have noticed them: they follow you about like tetchy trolls, hardly a day went by when I was in Russia without a brush with a museum attendant – 'Stand back!', 'Lower your voice!', 'That room is closed!', 'Where are your slippers? You must wear slippers!' – I can hear their querulous voices to this day, but I didn't ever try to get inside their heads. I was young, they were just there. In Paris I was old. In Paris they were impassive, immobile, barely distinguishable from the exhibits they were guarding. What in God's name did they think about all day, day after day, year after year, even decade after decade, sitting in almost total silence (just the odd clacking of heels on the parquet) inside that gloomy labyrinth, staring at the never-changing displays of artworks, maquettes and Gallo-Roman stones? Food? Sex? Their families in the suburbs? Their slavery? The point of all their days? Were they actually all slowly going mad? Did they ever start to hallucinate, to commune with wraiths from centuries past? That night I dreamt up Vassily: Musée Carnavalet out of Gogol.

By now over on Anzac Parade, alone in his museum, with Darya Gavrilovna, his punkish nemesis Boris and all the visitors gone for the day, Vassily will be in full swing, holding forth in his affably demented fashion about all the things that animate him, things simultaneously profound and trivial, as the things that the sanest of us are wrapped up in can be: in his case railways, the hope they offer, the great who passed through the town he lives in, Darya Gavrilovna (so 'amazingly supple of limb'), Norwegians (he never knows what to say to Norwegians), his cat Mr Pushkin . . . inconsequential things that at the same time make up his living core.

But that's all happening on Anzac Parade. Here in my bed on the tenth floor of St Vincent's, amongst those for whom the show is mostly (let's face it) over, I'm not 'on' at all. I'm quite alone. Stan and Ziggy have been curtained off for the night. And there's nobody sitting in the chair by my window this evening, either, because everyone I know is at the theatre.

I've scarcely ever been alone since I've been in this ward. Some friends drop in for a few minutes, some stay for an hour or two or, like Peter, for most of the day. 'Hullo!' they say with that special visiting-the-sick-in-hospital kind of awkwardness when they first come in. 'How are you feeling?' Why this embarrassment? (They can't really ask me how I *am*, after all, not on the tenth floor.) They often come with an offering – flowers sometimes, occasionally a book. The *National Geographic* is always a great favourite. 'You're a much better colour today!' they'll say encouragingly, smiling brightly. A bit of idle chit-chat, eyes wandering around the room, good wishes passed on from partners and mutual acquaintances, a few questions about the food and who else has been to see me. 'You're lucky to have this view,' they'll usually say at some point, admiring the panorama of skyscrapers to the west. I have no news, of course, because nothing is happening, and that makes conversation difficult. Who would want to know that this morning I used the lavatory for the first time? That, you see, is my really big news. I walked to the lavatory, sat on it and *went*.

The etiquette (at least in a cardiothoracic ward such as this one) is to bring you news from the outside world, as if you were a prisoner whose prospects for parole were best not touched upon. A couple of my more intimate friends are happy to just sit and keep me company. To them it's our being there together, in each other's presence, despite everything, that matters. I lie, they sit. We don't need news. We exchange presences.

What a strange ritual the hospital visit is, when you think about it! Yet it's somehow fundamental to our understanding of friendship and kindness.

For Jesus, for example, speaking of fundamentals, it was inseparable from being Good. For him visiting the sick was not just a kindness, but a blessèd thing to do – indeed, a soul-saving one. On Judgment Day, if I'm not mistaken, on his right hand will stand those who gave him something to eat and drink when he was hungry and thirsty, gave him clothes to put on when he was naked, and visited him when he was sick and in prison. (Not him, of course, not Jesus himself, as his disciples first thought, taking things literally again, as they were forever doing, but anyone we've met on the way, even the very least of them.) On his left, however, will stand those who gave him nothing to eat or drink, did not clothe him, and did not visit him when he was sick and in prison. They will be cast into everlasting fire. This now seems a bit over the top. He was about to be betrayed and killed when he made that threat, and knew it, so he was understandably a little overwrought, but all the same the punishment does not seem to fit the crime. In the quietness and half-dark I lie back and cogitate on what might have been at the heart of his fulminations.

Let's face it, this little diatribe is not about mere kindness – Christianity is not about being nice to each other, any more than Hinduism is, although it largely was in Lane Cove when I was a child. It's about seeing Truth face to face. Nothing is more irritating than hearing people who have not had a Christian thought pass through their heads since the day they were born declare that they are 'Christian' because they agree with that 'do unto others as you would have others do unto you' business, because they agree it's best to be nice to other people.

To be Good, be alert to how others you meet are experiencing the world – is that what Jesus meant? To be Good, go out of your way to put yourself in the shoes of others, unlock your heart as you look into theirs, and do whatever you can to ease their wretchedness. And in blessing you will be blessed. (A faint whiff of *darshan* here, oddly enough, don't you think?) It involves more, in other words, than simply turning up at someone's bedside with a bunch of glads and just five minutes to smile and nod before the meter runs out.

That said, I'm surprised at just how ill at ease some people can be during a hospital visit. At a loss for words, some even blush, while some talk too loudly, almost exuberantly, to cover feeling ill at ease. All the same, awkwardness is usually rustling around in there somewhere, like a nervous mouse. What gives rise to it?

It must be partly due to the sudden surge of real intimacy (perhaps unwanted or never felt before) in a room where, strangely, neither of you is at home, neither of you knows the rules or is sure about what comes next. As soon as you enter the ward you're confronted by a nakedness you're not accustomed to – not just uncovered skin and bones (although that, too), but utter nakedness, as you are when you come upon a man crying. You try to look away, as poor Essex must have done – remember that story? – when he burst in one day upon Elizabeth being put together in her bedchamber, to find her wigless, pox-scarred and hideously old.

'What a lovely view!' you exclaim. 'You can see the Opera House! Fantastic!' In front of you lies your friend's disturbingly *natural* self, as Essex might have thought of it once he'd composed himself, instead of his or her *clothed, performing* self. That's what intimacy is, after all: a disrobing, an unhurried disclosing over time, gradually or in little fits. It's comfortable intercourse with what you believe is someone's unadorned, natural self – but not, for the most part, quite so literally as this, of course. There's nothing comfortable about intercourse with my blotchy, skeletal self, lying here in this bed in my sagging, slightly smelly hospital pyjama top. Not (unlike Elizabeth) that I give a fig. The longer I lie here, the more shameless I feel.

I consider Elizabeth. Disconcertingly, since I'm feeling deeply theatrical tonight, I keep seeing in my mind's eye Dario Fo's Elizabeth, his grotesque, foul-mouthed bawd, growing madder by the minute on the last day of her life . . . what a play, what theatre, what abundant genius! . . . But something else is hovering in the wings, something quieter, something more . . . I know: Bacon (who actually had something to say himself about bodies natural and bodies . . . whatever the other kind is . . . political bodies, perhaps, performing bodies). Francis Bacon, loyal subject, chancellor of England (oh, it's flooding in now, my mind is jumping, it's a nest of squirrels, a pot of noodles on the boil) and coincidentally friend of the unfortunate Earl of Essex at one time, if I'm not mistaken, since Essex's name has come up, but not at the *wrong time*, as could so easily happen under the Tudors, and so consequently unlike Essex he kept his head (timing was everything for the upper crust) . . . also a homosexual, I seem to remember, just like the later Francis Bacon, the artist, I mean (speaking of foul-mouthed grotesques), a taste for adolescent boys, I think, but not boys of the same class, so it didn't count, but I'm no historian, I really don't know a thing about Bacon, he's actually a total blank . . . but anyway, Francis Bacon once paid tribute to his scarecrow queen,

Elizabeth, in the most elegant and revealing way: 'for assuredly,' he wrote, 'no person knoweth at any time the mind of another but in love. Love is the one window of the heart.' How beautifully put. The *one* window. Only when you love, according to Bacon, is the other's innermost being open to you – and yours to him. That's the heart of the matter, isn't it. That's intimacy.

A generation or so ago, I read somewhere, the average American had precisely 5.6 intimate friends and fifteen common and garden friends. The numbers have stuck in my mind. These days – and this is the sobering bit – the average is apparently just above zero. It's a sociological fact. Where I read it, though, has slipped my mind – certainly not in the Hobart *Mercury*. Perhaps I heard it on the ABC. Like conversation, it seems, intimacy in America is on the way out. I can't believe it's any better here. All that talk, all that tweeting and hooking up and liking on Facebook, but . . . no intimacy. Chat tweet chat tweet chat chat chat – we can't shut up, we natter away and message each other in broken English ceaselessly, but intimacy escapes us. It's a kind of spiritual destitution. I'm glad I was born when I was, I really am, all things considered.

How many intimate friends do I have – I mean, friends who are irreplaceable, friends whose wellbeing is vital to mine? Do I have 5.6? I stare at the black pane of glass across from my bed with the empty chair in front of it and consider my intimate loves. I have at least 5.6. Intimacy has come easily to me. In fact, for older generations, the problem is more how to deal with intimacies that over time have gone stale. Somerset Maugham put it perfectly in *Cakes and Ale* – a vicious little book, but you can't help liking it, I couldn't put it down – something about the common difficulty a man has as he grows older of coping with people he was once intimate with 'whose interest for him has in due course subsided'. 'Subsided' – it's a word that stays with you, it hits the nail on the head, no other word will quite do. It's natural – 'in due course' you change, they change, the setting changes and changes again, and you can no longer be bothered, either of you, paying attention to what matters deeply, or even shallowly, to the other, yet you can't find an agreed way to call it a day, nobody knows what the right ritual is for knocking the affair on the head and putting it out of its misery. By the time you get to my age, there are dozens of these exhausted intimacies hanging on, scarcely breathing, in cities around the globe. On the other hand, some intimacies, just a handful, two or three or four, never subside, they change with us.

Right now quite a few of the intimate friends I do have are in the theatre on Anzac Parade. What are Anthony and the gang up to at this moment? Has Turgenev, felled by a thunderbolt out of the blue (well, not quite out of the blue: he was at the theatre – and at the theatre, as we know, you're asking for it), fallen in love with Pauline Viardot yet? Has she sung that brilliant cavatina from *The Barber of Seville*? It snared him, that cavatina did, that night at the Opera in St Petersburg, it threw a noose around his heart – forever, that's the thing, making it hers until the day he died. Not the whole man, I hasten to say – he wasn't bound hand and foot – but his *heart*. (I've lost all sense of time, alone in this silent, dark corner of the universe. Has half an hour gone by? Five minutes?) Or has he by now been smitten by Marya Savina playing Vera in his own *Month in the Country* at the Alexandrinsky Theatre? (The theatre again, you see. Eros can't come out to play without art – lust can, lust can break out anywhere at all, lust can seize you by the throat in Coles, but not eros.) Savina did not snare his heart, however. This was infatuation, not love. At the end he felt like a buffoon. You do. But that won't happen until nearly ten o'clock. It can't be anywhere near ten o'clock yet, surely. Is it even nine? Is it interval?

An infatuation is not intimate. It craves intimacy, obviously; it is obsessed with intimacy, it dreams up an unending chain of intimacies, basking in breathless revelations and confessions, concocting ever more carnal storylines in its hunger to draw close. But it's too sudden, too one-sided to be truly intimate. Intimacy is woven delicately over time, it takes time to reach another's inmost self, and you need feelings that are returned.

'I have lost a treasure, such a Sister, such a friend as never can have been surpassed, – She was the sun of my life, the gilder of every pleasure, the soother of every sorrow, I had not a thought concealed from her, and it is as if I had lost a part of myself.'

Jane Austen's sister Cassandra on Jane's death

To lose an intimate friend forever brings not just immense sorrow but grief. And I think tenderly of those whose loss would cause me grief and who would in turn grieve for me. There are not many, not many at all – nor should there be. Some have been in this room with me today. At this moment, though, they are at the theatre, loving me in a completely different way.

And then there is Peter, who has my heart. He's there with them.

Stan cackles softly behind his curtain. Silence.

How inky black it is outside. The window beside my bed is like a sheet of black onyx. The glittering shafts of glass to the west make it seem even blacker.

I am wide awake.

All at once, here in this soundless, penumbral room, so still it could be a painting, I'm aware of beginning to eddy strangely.

Caught like a leaf in the shallows, I'm swivelling in slow motion on a turning tide.

223

Stock-still in my bed, I'm starting to float away from who I was just minutes ago. How very odd! I am transfixed.

With gathering speed, while not moving an inch, I'm drifting off, I'm being swept away. If any of my friends were sitting here by my bed, I'd be tempted to wave goodbye.

I'm not *dying* – well, only in general – I'm just facing away from . . . (it's hard to explain) . . . *from who I've always been*. I rather like the sensation. In the blink of an eye I've emerged on the other side of something, that's how it feels – into a pathless, blissfully pathless . . . (I can't think of the word, there must be a word) . . . *expanse*. How marvellously bracing! It's intoxicating, but at the same time I feel tranquil. Is this what ballooning on a fine morning feels like? For the first time in years, I feel untroubled by anything, anything at all.

'You see,' Jiddu Krishnamurti (who was a staunch advocate of pathlessness, by the way) once told a startled audience in California, 'I don't mind what happens.' So easy to be misunderstood when you say things like that. Now, I don't hold any particular candle for Krishnamurti – for that matter, Krishnamurti didn't hold any particular candle for himself, this being one of his disarming qualities – but I think I know what he meant. Since about three minutes ago, I don't mind what happens, either. Or I mind much less than I did this morning. It's an extraordinarily vivifying feeling, this not-minding-what-happens business. It quickens you. It makes me want to . . . I was going to say 'bang a tambourine', but that's not right at all . . . to sing, perhaps – it makes me want to sing. Something tethering me to my old self has snapped.

Thinking back, I had an inkling that the tide was turning a couple of weeks ago when I was mugged by death at midnight on that busy thoroughfare a few blocks away. I'd been thinking to myself for a while that I just wasn't *in the thick of it* any more and didn't yearn to be. It was dawning on me that not being in the thick of it – 'privacy', as Seneca calls it – is a kind of liberation to do exactly what I choose to do. The crowd that night just pranced on by like a street parade, banging its drums, as it were, and blowing its trumpets – well, of course it did, and so it should have, that's what crowds do, it will be doing it at this moment as I lie here. Curiously, though, it left me not so much abandoned by the wayside, staring wanly after it, as simply at rest to one side, not needing it any more in order to feel whole. And there are quite a few of us, I notice, now I take the trouble to look around me, ambling along by ourselves, no longer in the thick of it, looking oddly enlivened and refreshed, like certain monks you meet – not all, that goes without saying.

There was a time when we all thought we knew what it meant to live in the thick of it. At the very end of the talk I hurried to finish writing before catching the plane a couple of weeks ago, the one I'm supposed to give in a few months' time called 'Pushing Against the Dark', just before I take my bow and leave the stage, I will repeat, if I make it to November, the much-loved line from Gogol's comedy *The Government Inspector* with which the talk begins: the plea of a provincial landowner Pyotr Ivanovych Bobchinsky (a man who fails to exist to the point of being almost indistinguishable from his companion Pyotr Ivanovych Dobchinsky) to the rapacious nobody he mistakes for a government inspector just to mention his name, if his Excellency has the opportunity, to any bigwigs he might come across back in St Petersburg – even to the tsar himself, should he happen to be speaking to him. Just say, Bobchinsky counsels, 'in such-and-such a town lives Pyotr Ivanovych Bobchinsky. Just say that.' Bobchinsky and Dobchinsky are bewildered, discombobulated, as is my Vassily at first, by their insignificance in the wider world. Unseen, they have no being at all. We've all been versions of Bobchinsky and Dobchinsky in our time.

Well, we all want to *matter*, don't we. None of us wants the dark stealing over us as we grow older to blot out *mattering now*. We can't stave off time and nothingness forever, but we do want to matter *now*, today. It's not a question of living in the limelight, or being a celebrity, or changing the course of history, or even of being in the thick of it, but of mattering, of being of some account. To someone.

I don't, of course, give a damn about whether or not I've lived in the limelight or changed the course of anything, especially tonight, let alone about the bigwigs in the capital. You don't, not at moments like these, alone, high up in the sky at the end of the world, as the dark and the silence wrap themselves around you. Yet you do want to feel you matter. But to whom? Well, to those who matter to you, who else? That's enough. And I do feel I matter to a few people – intensely – and to one in particular, who is now, I imagine, watching the last act of my play, in which Vassily fails to matter to anybody at all except his cat, yet, being unhinged, is happy. That is my great attainment – not what I've said or written over the years, let alone this play of mine, which is of no account, when all is said and done – I know that, although it's been my delight for years – but mattering to people who matter to me. In this regard at least, if in no other, I have not lived in vain – and absolutely nobody wants to have done that.

There's a tinkle. 'Hullo? . . . Uhuh . . . Uhuh . . .' My smile is broadening. I think I'm starting to giggle. 'No, really? I can't believe it . . .' I'm chortling, I'm chuckling. 'They did?' I'm laughing soundlessly. My eyes are screwed tight with happiness. 'That's wonderful! Thank you . . . You, too . . . Yes, what a day, what a day . . . See you tomorrow.' (We never get lovey-dovey on the phone.)

Well, that didn't last long then, did it? One whiff of success and I'm *writhing* with pleasure in my bed. I suspect I might have just betrayed my new principles. Being in the thick of it is momentarily looking like quite an exciting prospect again.

But not really, though – who wouldn't be tickled pink to be applauded? The shift in my way of looking at the world is real. Sinking back into my pillows, I give a deep, contented sigh. Take love, for example. For many decades I was mostly trying to understand love in its various guises – affection, fondness, adoration, love-sickness, ardour, friendship, lust, tenderness and every other kind of attachment to another – or so it seems in retrospect. (Well, take this play of mine, for example.) I think that's what most of us do. All sorts of things grab our attention and rouse our passions as we grow older, but the underlying theme of life's first few acts is usually love. What is love? How many kinds of love are there? (There seem to be so confusingly, so astonishingly many.) How should I love? Why am I not more loved? Who can I love? 'Love one another.' 'God is love.' 'I love God and my country; I honour the flag; I serve my Queen . . .' *Je t'aime. Ich liebe Dich. Ti amo. Ya tebya lyublyu.* I can even say it in Finnish. Almost every song you sing to yourself from puberty onwards, every book you read and film you see year after year, is at least obliquely about seeking or finding love – not painting so much, I suppose, or at least not in the same way, but everything else, even the ballet in its high camp fashion. But Bacon was right, surely: love is just the window.

Now the tide has turned, I can feel my old eagerness to learn more and more about love falling away. Eros in particular, in the sense of a two-way hunger, is some-thing you have to leave behind when you're my age. I've pretty much learnt all I can cope with about loving.

Instead, I want to know the good ways to be old, there must be good ways, and also how to die – what days are for, in other words, when you're old and death is in the offing. I'd like to know more about good ways to be idle, too (not lazy or somnolent, but idle) – that, Seneca tells us, and he lived in a city where few reached old age (one in twenty at the most), is the key to making life feel long. I know enough about work, I need to learn how to be idle – not indolent, but idle, doing pleasurable things of my own choosing. It's something I've never been good at. I want to know more about valuing time as it glides past, too, about finding the days beautiful as they pass, despite everything. When you're still young, you no doubt have to give some thought to the shape of the years, to long-term goals, to real estate, to career trajectories, to balancing work and leisure, and to loving, but I don't. I don't want to be young or young at heart, nor do I want to be a prune-faced old toad, cornered in the cul-de-sac all lives end up in. I just want to be old in a good way. I want to move from the outer to the inner. It's not a matter of 'not going gentle' or 'going gentle' into that good night, or raging against the dying of the light, as the young Dylan Thomas would have it in his poem for his dying father; at least not for me at the age I am – in fact, to be honest, I find the whole poem jejune. Why rage? It's a matter of loving, each day, what you have been and what and who you have given your heart to. Seneca says the trick is to bring all the different times together in one moment: to embrace the past in recollection, to use the present wisely and to anticipate with pleasure what is to come. It's a lot to ask. Do I have the strength?

'What is to come' . . . I remember something that Pico Iyer once wrote about beauty: it's in their passing that a good part of the beauty of most things lies. Yet it's not until you're at least middle-aged (as Pico himself now is) that you have the leisure to treasure the beauty passing time creates. Calling a spade a spade, as he likes to do, in a letter about Japan, which is where he lives, Pico once wrote to me that 'the beauty of *everything* here lies entirely in its mortality'. It's a fearless thing to say. I must try to be braver.

Perhaps, I reflect, gazing at the silent, brilliantly moonlit city to the west, it's only now, with my life the shape it is (for good or ill), that I can savour the passing time, delighting in the luxury of asking nothing more than to be happy in each intricately layered day. I agree with André Gide, by the way, not the Buddhists, about happiness: happiness is learning to desire only what you can have. It's knowing what to do with your freedom. It's not bliss, of course, but it *is* happiness.

∼∾

I feel time's fingers ease their grip on my throat and I smile. At last – *at last* – I can wheel and swoop about inside the spiritual city that is my mind, going absolutely nowhere, having the time of my life.